A Travel ✦ Guide to

The
Plantation
South

By Jim Gullo

LUCENT BOOKS

An imprint of Thomson Gale, a part of The Thomson Corporation

THOMSON
✦ ™
GALE

Detroit • New York • San Francisco • San Diego • New Haven, Conn. • Waterville, Maine • London • Munich

LIBRARY OF CONGRESS CATALOGING-IN-PUBLICATION DATA

Gullo, Jim, 1957–
  The plantation South / by Jim Gullo.
    p. cm. — (A travel guide to)
Includes bibliographical references and index.
  Contents: A brief history of the South—The geography and climate of the South—
  Getting to the South—Visiting plantations—Exploring rural Southern culture
  Exploring the South's major cities.
  ISBN 1-59018-360-6 (hard cover : alk. paper)
  1. Plantation life—Southern States—History—19th century—Juvenile literature. 2.
Southern States—Social life and customs—1775–1865—Juvenile literature. 3. Slaves—
Southern States—Social conditions—19th century—Juvenile literature. 4. Southern
States—Guidebooks—Juvenile literature. I. Title. II. Series: Travel guide (Lucent Books)
F213.G86 2005
975'.03—dc22

                                                                    2004023415

Printed in the United States of America

0531

Contents

Foreword

Travel can be a unique way to learn about oneself and other cultures. The esteemed American writer and historian, John Hope Franklin, poetically expressed his conviction in the value of travel by urging, "We must go beyond textbooks, go out into the bypaths and untrodden depths of the wilderness and travel and explore and tell the world the glories of our journey." The message communicated by this eloquent entreaty is clear: The value of travel is to temper one's imagination about a place and its people with reality, and instead of thinking how things may be, to be able to experience them as they really are.

Franklin's voice is not alone in his summons for students to "travel and explore." He is joined by a stentorian chorus of thinkers that includes former president John F. Kennedy, who established the Peace Corps to facilitate cross-cultural understandings between Americans and citizens of other lands. Ideas about the benefits of travel do not spring only from contemporary times. The ancient Greek historian Herodotus journeyed to foreign lands for the purpose of immersing himself in unfamiliar cultural traditions. In this way, he believed, he might gain a first-hand understanding of people and ways of life in other places.

The joys, insights, and satisfaction that travelers derive from their journeys are not limited to cultural understanding. Travel has the added value of enhancing the traveler's inner self by expanding his or her range of experiences. Writer Paul Tournier concurs that, "The real meaning of travel, like that of a conversation by the fireside, is the discovery of oneself through contact with other people."

The Lucent Books Travel Guide series enlivens history by introducing a new and innovative style and format. Each volume in the series presents the history of a preeminent historical travel destination written in the casual style and format of a travel guide. Whether providing a tour of fifth-century B.C. Athens, Renaissance Florence, or Shakespeare's London, each book describes a city or area at its cultural peak and orients readers to only those places and activities that are known to have existed at that time.

A high level of authenticity is achieved in the Travel Guide series. Each book is written in the present tense and addresses the reader as a prospective foreign traveler. The sense of authenticity is further achieved, whenever possible, by the inclusion of descriptive quotations by contemporary writers who knew the place; information on fascinating historical sites; and travel tips meant to explain unusual cultural idiosyncrasies that give depth and texture to all great cultural centers. Even shopping details, such as where to buy an ermine-trimmed gown, or a much-needed house slave, are included to inform readers of what items were sought after throughout history.

Looked at collectively, this series presents an appealing presentation of many of the cultural and social highlights of Western civilization. The collection also provides a framework for discussion about the larger historical currents that dominated not only each travel destination but countries and entire continents as well. Each book is customized by the author to bring to the fore the most important and most interesting characteristics that define each title. High standards of scholarship are assured in the series by the generous peppering of relevant quotes and extensive bibliographies. These tools provide readers a scholastic standard for their own research as well as a guide to direct them to other books, periodicals, and Web sites that will provide them greater breadth and detail.

A Culture All Its Own

I found that the South one reads and hears of is altogether different from the one that one sees and becomes acquainted with.

—A. De Puy Van Buren of Battle Creek, Michigan, after spending a year in Yazoo County, Mississippi, in the 1850s

To all of our readers, we bid a most gracious welcome. The South of the 1850s has never been more lovely or welcoming, nor has it been more prosperous. This guidebook will lead you to a region of the United States where the climate is warm and agreeable throughout the year; where nature is on display in a dazzling array of woods, swamps, scenic rivers, and great rolling tracts of farmland; and where people are friendly, and the qualities of hospitality and gentility are considered to be great virtues.

Southern culture is charming and interesting, and you may be surprised by how much everything—from the food to the language—challenges your expectations. The region is growing and changing so quickly that your preconceived notions of Southern life and society will almost certainly be tested.

Do you think that the great mansions of America are concentrated in New York City or Boston? In the South, there are areas where the mansions are lined up one after another for a hundred miles, and each one vies to be the grandest and most opulently appointed. Southerners who are becoming fabulously wealthy on the goods that they grow and sell are proud to display their wealth. The knowledgeable visitor may be invited to share in this affluence at a plantation party and the lucky visitor may even be asked to stay as a guest.

Do you still believe that America's liveliest cities are located only in the

North? The South's cities are growing and becoming important centers of commerce, education, and culture. Richmond and Charleston, the respective capitals of Virginia and South Carolina, are important seats of government and industry. Savannah is Georgia's lovely port city, and New Orleans, with its French influence and lively society, is a vital center for shipping the goods that travel down the Mississippi River. (Even if you are not a "city person," your travels will almost certainly touch upon cities, for they are the junctures and transfer points for almost all transportation in the region.) In each metropolitan area you may be astonished to encounter the great bustle of commerce; lovely parks and stately architecture in both the residential and commercial sections; and the liveliest of cultural scenes, with societies devoted to opera, classical music, and theater. Many of the finest hotels and restaurants in America are located in Southern cities, with appointments and menus as sophisticated as any in the North and East.

Despite the focus on business, the spirit of the South is unlike anything you may have experienced. Certainly to

The banks of the Mississippi River are lined with a number of elegant plantation homes like this one featuring tall trees draped with Spanish moss.

A line of slaves carries sacks of cotton on their heads after they return from a day of picking on a South Carolina plantation.

anyone used to the bustle and frenetic pace of a big city, the relaxed pace and gentle rhythms of Southern life may be the greatest surprise of all. "It is an indolent, yet charming life, and one quits thinking and takes to dreaming,"[1] writes John Anthony Quitman, a young New Yorker who moved to Natchez, Mississippi, in the 1820s.

The Land of Cotton and Profits

At this midcentury juncture, cotton and sugar are king, and planters are making fortunes by developing new and more economical ways to grow, process, and deliver crops and their products to mar-

kets the world over. The South has been in a cycle of unprecedented growth and prosperity for the last three decades, thanks in large part to Eli Whitney's cotton gin, which revolutionized the speed and efficiency with which cotton could be processed. Of the more than 3.8 million bales of cotton that are produced each year in the South, nearly two-thirds are exported, forming the major portion of the world's supply. In just the last two years, Texas alone has shipped 116,078 bales of high-quality cotton. Quitman notes:

The planters are the prominent feature [of southern society]. They ride fine horses, are followed by well-dressed and very aristocratic servants. . . . They live profusely; drink costly Port, Madeira, and sherry . . . and are exceedingly hospitable. Cotton-planting is the most lucrative business that can be followed. Some of the planters net $50,000 from a single crop.[2]

Cotton

The South's other staple crops—Virginia tobacco, Carolina rice, Louisiana sugar, and corn from every corner—continue to thrive. The South feeds not only itself, but the nation. In the summertime, for example, nearly twenty-five hundred barrels of potatoes are shipped every month from Norfolk to Philadelphia and New York City, as well as three hundred to five hundred barrels of cucumbers and muskmelons. In addition, the South supplies much of the country with important commodities such as the shingles from North Carolina that roof the homes of New England, and coal from Virginia that fuels the nation's manufacturing furnaces and locomotives.

Whistling Dixie

The new song sweeping the South, "Dixie (I Wish I Was in Dixie Land)," is quickly becoming an anthem for the entire region. Written by Daniel Decatur Emmett on a cold, dreary day in New York City, it perfectly captures the nostalgic love of the South that many Southerners feel. You will hear it played not once, but repeatedly, at just about any concert or recital of popular music. The lyrics are written in a Negro patois that is popular with today's minstrels.

I wish I was in land ob cotton,
Old times dar am not forgotten.
Look away! Look away!
Look away! Dixie Land.

In Dixie Land whar' I was born in,
Early on one frosty mornin',
Look away! Look away!
Look away! Dixie Land.

CHORUS:

Den I wish I was in Dixie,
Hooray! Hoo-ray!
In Dixie Land, I'll take my stand
to lib and die in Dixie;

Away, away, away
down south in Dixie,
Away, away, away
down south in Dixie.

Lumber and flour production are at historic levels, and for the first time ever, Southerners have begun to ship their products directly to Europe from ships that sail from Virginia. The South produces vast quantities of railroad iron in places like Cumberland, Maryland, and the Virginia cities of Wheeling and Richmond. Richmond is also manufacturing locomotives. New roads are being built at unprecedented levels, and railroad tracks have increased their mileage five-fold in the South in the last twenty years.

Southern Society

During your travels, you will encounter great poverty as well as great wealth. The South is rapidly becoming a four-class society. At the top are the small class of wealthy plantation owners who control nearly self-sufficient estates. "A Southern plantation, well managed, had nearly everything necessary to life done within its bounds,"[3] writes Susan Dabney Smedes of her childhood on a Mississippi plantation. Besides their cash crops, they grow almost all of their own food, raise enough hogs to feed perhaps hundreds of plantation workers, build and maintain mills for refining their products, and establish subsidiary services such as blacksmithing, machining, and home construction. They are also the unofficial ambassadors of Southern goodwill, offering hospitality to dozens of travelers, relatives, and visiting dignitaries each year.

In the middle of Southern society are hardworking yeoman farmers who tend their own plots of land and are also largely self-sufficient. Most live simply in log cabins that have their own distinctive features to accommodate the Southern climate of cool winters and hot summers. They too are valuable resources for the traveler: You will depend on them for many a meal and bed for the night during your journey through the South.

Near the bottom of Southern society are the "crackers" or "hillbillies"—poor rural whites who live in miserable poverty and ignorance, eking out meager livings from the soil; and below them are the millions of slaves who provide the daily labor that keeps the Southern economy viable.

Slavery and the South

Slavery is a legal practice in the southern United States. Both whites and free blacks have the right to buy, own, and sell slaves. Regardless of your personal opinions on the institution, keep in mind during your travels that slavery is deeply ingrained and strongly defended by white slave owners. You will find that slavery is an issue that is almost continually discussed throughout the South, both during your visits to plantation homes and during casual conversations with strangers on boats, trains, and stagecoaches. Southerners are aware of the controversy over slavery outside the region and are generally offended by rebukes, though reasonable discussion may be possible.

Slavery is simply a fact of Southern life. As one slave owner said recently, "It was not instituted by us—we are not responsible for it. It is unfortunately fixed upon us; we could not do away with it if we wished; our duty is only to make the best of a bad thing; to lessen its evils as much as we can."[4]

If you are curious about slaves, you will have plenty of opportunities to interact with them. Slaves travel with their masters on the same boats and trains as you will take, even riding in the same railroad cars. The strict segregation that is practiced in the North in this regard is far more relaxed in the South when slaves are accompanied by their masters. Slaves will often be your stewards in hotels, and will cook and serve food for you in plantation homes.

You may encounter more startling sights. You will probably travel on ships alongside groups of Negroes in chains and manacles who are being trans-ported to the Deep South states of Alabama, Louisiana, and Mississippi. You may see men and women being whipped. You will often read advertisements in the newspapers from slave owners seeking help in returning runaway slaves, as well as announcements for upcoming sales of slaves.

Bring Your Best Manners

You will find that Southerners are eager to meet with you and display the hospitality that has become synonymous with

A young Southern belle and her slave shop in a market. Slaves not only work the fields, but many perform household chores for their owners.

the South. You will be introduced to exotic foods like grits, ashcakes, chitterlings, and (if you are very lucky) spooncake and sweet potato pie. You will hear the music of the banjo and the fiddle and the Negro spiritual. You will see profusions of flowers and experience warm weather even in the dead of winter. You will be treated to numerous simple pleasures (one English traveler was delighted and surprised to find herself eating fresh green peas in March, fully three months before they appear on Northern tables).

Try to bring your best manners and respond as graciously as Southerners respond to you. Southern gentlemen exhibit a chivalry based in the courtly life of England and France, and Southern women attempt to be paragons of virtue and grace. Southerners revere the gentle voice and a peaceful nature. The South is undergoing enormous change. Wealth and poverty, tradition and modernization are in sometimes uneasy juxtaposition. See for yourself all of the wonders and contradictions of the South as you set out to explore the region.

Chapter 1

A Brief History of the South

Before the Europeans arrived in the New World, the South was inhabited by Native American tribes. Creeks and Choctaws, Croatans and Apalachees, Cherokees, Seminoles, and Tuscaroras all claimed parts of the South as their tribal lands. They lived together, if not amicably, in a stasis that was broken only when explorers began to arrive from Europe. The explorers were soon followed by settlers who sent back reports of a land that was "the most plentiful, sweete, fruitful and wholesome of all the worlde,"[5] as one English settler ecstatically noted in a letter home.

Searching for Cities of Gold

The first Europeans to explore the land that we now know as the South were Spanish explorers and conquerors in the early sixteenth century. They came seeking riches and supernatural rewards. Juan Ponce de Leon, the governor of Puerto Rico, explored the coast of Florida in 1513. His quest was to find a reputed fountain and river that could make older men young, and a city of gold. He searched for his "fountain of youth" for eight years before dying at the hands of hostile Native Americans.

Other explorers and conquistadores came looking for even more exotic treasures. One group explored what is now South Carolina in a vain search for a mythical civilization that one Native American claimed was a land of pearls, giant kings, domesticated deer, and men with inflexible tails, which they used as seats. In 1539, Spaniard Hernando de Soto entered Florida with an army of men who wore full suits of armor and rode armored horses. With them they carried iron collars and chains in

Ponce de Léon was one of the first Europeans to explore the North American mainland. He spent eight years in Florida searching in vain for a "fountain of youth."

"Logan Is the Friend of White Men"

Not all Indians or tribes were enemies of America's early settlers. In his landmark book, *Notes on the State of Virginia*, which was published in 1787, Thomas Jefferson quotes this speech by Logan, a Mingo chief whose family was killed by white settlers:

> I appeal to any white man to say, if ever he entered Logan's cabin hungry, and he gave him not meat; if ever he came cold and naked, and he clothed him not. During the course of the last long and bloody war, Logan remained idle in his cabin, an advocate for peace. Such was my love for the whites that my countrymen pointed as they passed, and said, "Logan is the friend of white men." I had even thought to have lived with you, but for the injuries of one man, Col. Cresap, the last spring, in cold blood, and unprovoked, murdered all the relations of Logan, not sparing even my women and children. There runs not a drop of my blood in the veins of any living creature. This called on me for revenge.

hopes of enslaving the natives. With promises of finding settlements of gold so rich that the men wore golden hats, de Soto made his way across the Savannah River, through upper Georgia and Alabama, and west across the Mississippi River near the site of present-day Memphis. He never found the city of gold, but he did become the first European to cross the mighty river. His expedition ended, weary and ravaged by attacks, at the Gulf of Mexico four years after it began.

In 1565, the Spanish Crown sent a fierce naval commander named Pedro Menendez to destroy a French settlement on the coast of Florida. Menendez was successful and renamed the village St. Augustine. The town was razed by British sailor Sir Francis Drake a year later. Menendez went on to establish a series of outposts from Tampa Bay to South Carolina, and even had a settlement planned for the Chesapeake Bay. At the same time, despite fierce, unrelenting attacks by local tribes, groups of Jesuit and Franciscan missionaries attempted to erect missions in present-day Florida, Georgia, and South Carolina.

The first English settlement in North America came in 1587, when Sir Walter Raleigh sent colonists to Roanoke Island, off the coast of North Carolina, under the leadership of John White. White returned to England for supplies a few years later, and when he returned to America in 1590, the colony had vanished, including his newly born granddaughter, Virginia Dare. A single mysterious word carved onto a tree—"Croatoan"—was the only clue as to the fate of what became known as "The Lost Colony of Roanoke."

English settlers come ashore in Virginia in 1607. Their settlement, Jamestown, eventually failed, as colonists fell prey to disease, starvation, and Indian attacks.

Jamestown Landing and Settlement

In 1607, an ambitious plan to settle the New World was conceived in England. A group called the Virginia Company launched three ships with more than a hundred men who were bound for Virginia. They landed at a marshy island on the Chesapeake Bay, and they named their settlement Jamestown.

At first, the unspoiled new land seemed like paradise. Wrote one settler named George Percy, "We found nothing worth speaking of but faire meadows and goodly tall Trees, with such Fresh waters running through woods as I was almost ravished at the first sight thereof. . . . [There were] many squirrels, conies, Black Birds with crimson wings, and divers other Fowls and Birds of divers and sundrie colours."[6] Percy went on to describe great stands of cedar and cypress trees, and wild strawberries that were four times larger than the ones he had known in England.

Jamestown, however, was not a success. More colonists were sent from England, including women who married and began to produce children in the New World, but by 1624, only 1,275 of 6,000 colonists had survived. They died of disease in the marshy, humid climate, and of their own ignorance in survival skills, such as lack of rudimentary knowledge of hunting, fishing, and farming. They also died of Indian attacks, despite the colo-nists' naive intentions to bring Christianity to the native population. In 1622, fierce attacks by the local tribes killed one-quarter of the colonial population, and from then on the colonists adopted a policy of fighting and attacking the native tribes that were trying to drive them from the land.

Colonial Times

The colony at Jamestown, despite its severe hardships and deprivation, did establish that crops could successfully be grown on southern soil. The original

Jamestown colonists suffered exceptional hardships for years. Here a father passes out the remaining few kernels of corn during a time of want.

The Plantation South

cash crop of Virginia, and of the South, was tobacco, which the Native Americans smoked from long-stemmed pipes with stone bowls. The practice of smoking became such an instant fashion in England that by 1624 Virginia was exporting sixty thousand pounds a year of the addictive leaf. It was a huge source of revenue for the colonies.

English settlements began to expand slowly up and down the Atlantic sea-board. In 1632, an English peer named Lord Baltimore was granted title to more than 10 million acres in the region that would become Maryland. Two years later, he sailed two ships with more than two hundred immigrants aboard and settled an area of the Potomac River, 70 miles (114km) north of Jamestown, known as St. Mary's. These colonists were more successful with bartering and trading with the local tribes, as well as with

Slaves work the fields of a tobacco plantation in Virginia. Jamestown colonists quickly learned that tobacco, a very lucrative crop, was well suited to Southern soil.

Southern Statesmen

The South has had many great statesmen and leaders during our country's seventy five-year history. Four of the first five presidents of the United States came from Virginia, beginning with George Washington and continuing with Thomas Jefferson, James Madison, and James Monroe, the country's third, fourth, and fifth presidents, respectively. "Old Hickory" (the nickname given to popular President Andrew Jackson), was born in the Carolinas and began his political career in Tennessee, and President Zachary Taylor, who died in office in 1850, grew up in Kentucky. In the present administration of President Franklin Pierce, Mississippi's Jefferson Davis is the secretary of war, and Virginia's Robert E. Lee serves with distinction as a General of the Army.

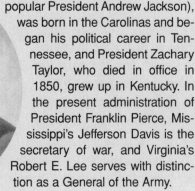

Thomas Jefferson

farming the land and providing themselves with food, water, and adequate shelter. Their settlement thrived even as Jamestown struggled and would eventually be abandoned.

At the same time of the Jamestown settlement, the French had established a presence in Quebec, Canada, and during the last years of the seventeenth century, they began to move south along the Mississippi River. In 1699, a French settlement was established in present-day Biloxi on the Gulf of Mexico. Natchitoches was established in 1713 as the first settlement in present-day Louisiana, which was closely followed by Natchez (1716) and New Orleans (1718). Four years after its founding, New Orleans became the capital of the new territory of Louisiana.

North Carolina was also settled by Europeans. Quakers moved in and were granted land; French Huguenots founded the town of Bath; and Swiss and German immigrants founded the town of New Bern. Settlements pushed to Cape Fear, and thriving businesses in tobacco, lumber, tar, pitch, and turpentine from the region's extensive pine forests provided the financial incentive for more immigrants to settle the region. Farther south, the confluence of the Ashley and Cooper rivers provided the site for a new settlement in the 1670s that became Charleston, which in 1680 was named the seat of government of South Carolina.

Where the Europeans arrived, the trappings of civilization quickly followed. Local governments were established; fields were cleared and farms were created; trees were felled and homes were built, some predating the rich mansions that the South now knows; and churches and schools were erected. Native American tribes that had once roamed the land were either engaged in battle, pushed beyond the boundaries of the colonies, or forced into uneasy truces as they saw more and more of their land seized. By 1713, for example, the Tuscarora tribe that had once fiercely held its ground on the eastern seaboard, was driven out of North Carolina for good. Its people were forced to move west and fend for themselves. Conflicts with the Seminole Indians in Florida and the Cherokees of Georgia have ceased in the last twenty years, ending centuries of hostilities between white settlers and Native Americans.

Rich in Natural Resources

The early colonists quickly discovered that their new home was abundant in natural resources. In a catalog of "blessings" written in 1705, Englishman Robert Beverley described extensive meadows "wherein are hundreds of acres without any Tree at all [covered in] Grass of Incredible Height." He wrote of finding vast deposits of coal, iron ore, and lead, and of trees that grow "at every Man's Door so fast, that after it has been cut down, it will in Seven Years time, grow up again from Seed, to substantial Firewood."[7]

Thirty years before Beverley's book appeared, other explorers in Virginia's Appalachian mountain region wrote of encountering vast numbers of wild turkeys, and deer, elk, and buffalo that had no natural fear of Man. Kentucky in the eighteenth century was a rugged, wild place of rushing rivers that cut swaths through limestone canyons, catfish that weighed as much as one hundred pounds coexisting with forty-pound salmon, and wildlife that included teeming numbers of bears, beavers, muskrats, otters, mink, panthers, wolves, and even parakeets.

In the early 1700s, another Englishman, named John Lawson, set out to explore the area that is now the border between North and South Carolina. He published a book with the lengthy title, *A New Voyage to Carolina; Containing an Exact Description and Natural History of that Country; Together with the Present State thereof and a Journal of a Thousand Miles, Travel'd thro several Nations of Indians, giving a particular Account of their Customs, Manners, etc.*, wherein he described forests of giant cypress trees, flocks of wild turkeys, and enormous numbers of passenger pigeons that filled the skies. The pigeons, he wrote, were "so numerous in these Parts, that you might see Millions in a Flock; they sometimes split off the Limbs of stout Oaks . . . upon which they roost o' Nights."[8]

Lawson also met and befriended the Waxhaw tribe, whose people were described as tall, straight Indians who had flattened their heads in front and back by bindings when they were infants. This caused their eyes to protrude dramatically and gave them a frightening appearance.

Studies of the South's great natural history continue into modern times. Just three decades ago, in 1820, the noted ornithologist John James Audubon embarked on a boat journey from Cincinnati to New Orleans where he observed millions of native birds, including bald eagles, flocks of teal and sandhill cranes, swarms of grackles and purple finches, and, at the confluence of the Mississippi and Yazoo rivers, ducks and geese by the thousands, and millions of cormorants.

The Slave Trade Begins

The Portuguese had begun to enslave Africans at the end of the fifteenth century, mostly to work in the hardwood

This magnificent print of a blue heron preening its feathers was created by the noted ornithologist John James Audubon during his recent expedition down the Mississippi River.

forests of the Portuguese colony of Brazil. As the islands of the Americas were conquered and it was discovered that sugar thrived in the Caribbean climate, more slaves were captured and sent to the islands of Jamaica, Cuba, Barbados, and others to work in the labor-intensive sugar plantations. By 1550, the Dutch, the French, the English, Swedes, Danes, and Prussians had all joined Portugal in establishing forts on Africa's west coast for the purpose of purchasing or capturing slaves and shipping them across the Atlantic Ocean.

AFRICA

Slavery was relatively slow to come to America and the South. A group of twenty Africans were sent to Jamestown

in 1619 as indentured servants. They worked for seven years to earn their freedom, and continued to live in the colony as freemen. By 1699, however, all blacks were declared to be slaves in Virginia. By that time, the labor needs of growing tobacco in Virginia, and the new crops of rice and indigo in the Carolinas, dictated the needs of planters to use slave labor. By 1754, there were fifteen thousand slaves in the Carolinas. Georgia, which was founded and settled in 1733 as a haven for immigrants from Scotland and Germany, resisted slavery for more than twenty years. No slaves were allowed in the colony until 1755, but pressure to introduce slaves came from newly arrived planters who were eager to cultivate the land with cash crops. By 1760, there were six thousand slaves in Georgia. By that time, England had become the largest trader of slaves in the world, delivering forty-five thousand slaves a year to the New World by the close of the eighteenth century.

Initially, most American slaves came from the coast of West Africa from the areas of Senegambia, Sierra Leone, the Bight of Biafra, and the Bight of Benin. For the most part, the slaves were tribesmen who had been captured by other Africans and sold to the Europeans. The need for slave labor became so acute that traders had to search farther afield for captives. From 1733 to 1807,

When Southern States Were Formed

Of the thirteen states to ratify the U.S. Constitution in 1788–1789, five were from the South: Georgia, Maryland, North Carolina, South Carolina, and Virginia. The remaining Southern states, and the years that they joined the Union, are Kentucky (1792), Tennessee (1796), Louisiana (1812), Mississippi (1817), Alabama (1819), Missouri (1821), Arkansas (1836), and Florida (1845).

Armed colonists stand guard over the first slaves brought to Jamestown in 1619. Although these slaves became freedmen, by the eighteenth century all blacks in Virginia became slaves for life.

Patrick Henry speaks out against the tyranny of British rule before members of the Virginia Assembly. It was during this address that Henry declared, "Give me liberty or give me death."

40 percent of the Africans who were imported to South Carolina were Angolans from the central and southern parts of Africa.

By 1807, slavery in the South was so firmly established that slave families were reproducing quickly enough to supply a steady stream of labor for the growing agricultural needs of the region. That year, the United States outlawed the importation of new slaves, and the sight of ships arriving loaded with slaves from Africa ended.

South During the Revolutionary War

By the middle of the eighteenth century, southern colonies were joining their northern counterparts in chafing at British rule. They objected to the taxes imposed on their crops and goods by the British government, and they objected to British rules against westward expansion by American colonies. Virginians in particular had developed a sense of independence that was noticeable to the visitor of the 1760s. One British man wrote:

The Virginians are haughty and jealous of their liberties, impatient of restraint, and can scarcely bear the thought of being controlled by any superior power. Many of them consider the colonies as independent states, not connected with Great Britain, otherwise than by having the same common King, and being bound to her [Great Britain] by natural affection.[9]

Revolts against the British leadership began to break out throughout the South in 1775. In March of that year, a fiery orator from Virginia named Patrick Henry declared, "Give me liberty or give me death." The British-appointed governor of Virginia was forced to escape from Williamsburg two months later under threat of death by a local militia; within six months, the Crown-appointed governors of North Carolina, South Carolina, and Georgia did the same. It was Thomas Jefferson, a Virginia statesman, scholar, and planter (and slave owner), who drafted the Declaration of Independence that was ratified by the Continental Congress in Philadelphia in July 1776.

Fighting in the South was sporadic during the war that followed. A group of patriots fought and won a battle at

Travel Tip: How the Fugitive Slave Act Affects You

The Fugitive Slave Act of 1850 makes it a federal crime to assist runaway slaves. As a traveler, be aware that you can be prosecuted in both the Southern and the Northern states if you knowingly help a slave who is seeking to escape his masters, or if you obstruct a federal official who is searching for runaway slaves.

Moore's Creek Bridge in North Carolina in 1776. British ships were attacked and sunk in Savannah Harbor, but by 1778, the British seized control of Savannah. Two years later, the city of Charleston, South Carolina, was also captured and returned to British rule until the end of the war. The final battle of the war took place in Yorktown, Virginia, in the fall of 1781, when General George Washington's army joined with French troops to defeat the British army under the command of Lord Charles Cornwallis.

Expansion westward continued after the war, as the territories of Kentucky and Tennessee were settled. Thomas Jefferson's Louisiana Purchase from the French in 1803 doubled the size of the United States, and added the lands along the lower Mississippi River to the South's portion of the growing country.

The Compromise of 1850

The South has enjoyed a prolonged period of peace and prosperity since the War of 1812 ended with the British defeat at New Orleans in 1815. Conflict of another kind arose at the beginning of this decade when some Southern states threatened to secede from the Union if their concerns regarding slavery were not heard in Washington, D.C. President Zachary Taylor, a hero of the Mexican-American War who was

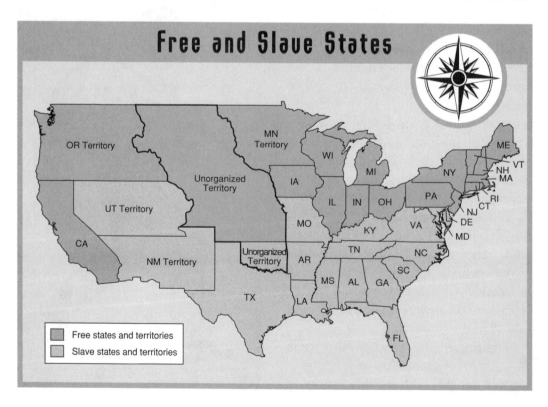

Free and Slave States

himself a Southern plantation owner, threatened to keep the union together by force. There were rumblings of a possible Civil War between the Northern and the Southern states over the issue. Shortly after Taylor's death in office in 1850, however, Southern politicians brokered a complex compromise between the slave-holding Southern states and free Northern states over several land and slavery issues. Southern states were satisfied with a new law called the Fugitive Slave Act that has made it a federal crime to harbor runaway slaves in any part of the United States. The Compromise of 1850, as it is known, preserved the union and peace between the North and South.

Chapter 2

The Geography and Climate of the South

The South begins at the Mason-Dixon Line, the surveyors' boundary line, completed in 1767, that is the southern boundary of Pennsylvania and the western boundary of Delaware. Territory south of that, all the way to the Gulf of Mexico, is the U.S. South. The east-west boundaries of the South are the Atlantic Ocean and the Mississippi River, respectively. Beyond the mighty river to the west are the southwest states of Texas and California, as well as vast lands stretching to the Pacific Ocean that are officially designated as U.S. territories.

The traveler might view the South as a vast square of land with roughly equal sides. At its widest point, between the Atlantic Ocean seaport of Norfolk, Virginia, and the Mississippi River, the South measures approximately 900 miles (1,448km), tapering down to just over 500 miles (805km) between Jacksonville, Florida, and New Orleans, Louisiana. From a north-south perspective, the distance between Baltimore, Maryland, and Miami, Florida, is just over 1,000 miles (1,609km).

The South's Subregions

You could spend a lifetime exploring the South and never see all of it. Deciding how to spend your time and budget can be difficult. Will you visit Southern cities or agricultural zones? Would you prefer to explore mountainous areas or remote islands? An understanding of the South's three major subregions can help guide you as you plan your trip. They comprise mountains, coastal areas, and agricultural regions. The boundaries of most Southern states have been laid over some combination of the three.

If you want to visit the very source of the South's wealth and economic base, you will head for the Deep South, also known as the Cotton Belt, which extends roughly from eastern North Carolina through South Carolina and across a long swath of Georgia, Alabama, Mississippi, and Louisiana, ending finally in eastern Texas. This is the South's most fertile agricultural land and the home to its largest farms and plantations. Indeed, the soil is so rich here that it is sometimes referred to as the Black Belt for its deep color and ability to grow crops. Life in this part of the South revolves around the growing, harvesting, processing, and delivery of crops and agricultural products, and much of your time in the Cotton Belt will be spent visiting plantations and experiencing the gentle rhythms of the farming life.

The Piedmont is the name given to the area of the South that comprises the eastern foothills of the Appalachian Mountains to the Atlantic Coast. With gently rolling hills and abundant water, the Piedmont encompasses some of the southeast's major cities, including Richmond, Charlotte, Atlanta, and Birmingham. Your travels here will be equal parts rural and urban, as you move between areas of farmland and the South's major cities. These cities are the hubs of culture, commerce, and in the case of coastal

Here we see a typical cotton plantation of the Deep South. The warm, damp climate of the Deep South creates ideal conditions for growing cotton and other cash crops.

The Mason-Dixon Line

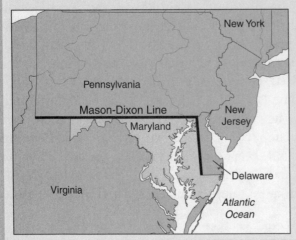

Where does the South officially begin and end in relation to the states of the North? The answer lies in the work of two English surveyors, Charles Mason and Jeremiah Dixon, who set out in 1763 to settle a property dispute and ended up setting the border between the neighboring states of Pennsylvania and Maryland. Using astronomic readings, the two men worked for four years to determine a geographic boundary that officially rests at 39°43'19.521' north latitude. This line on the maps of the era became known as the Mason-Dixon Line, and it has since been used as a convenient way to separate the North from the South. In other words, for the purposes of a traveler, once you cross the Mason-Dixon Line, you are officially in the South, or Dixie, as it is popularly called.

cities like Savannah and Charleston, shipping, as the goods of the South are consolidated and sent off to markets in Europe and northern U.S. cities.

The Southern Highlands are hilly, remote areas of the South that have their own distinctive culture and landscapes. These are the steeper slopes of the Appalachians, that great backbone of mountain ranges that stretches from Georgia all the way north to Maine and provides the tallest peaks in the United States. The highlands include the Ozarks region of northern Arkansas and southern Missouri, as well as Appalachian communities of Virginia, Tennessee, and parts of northern Georgia. Travel here is arduous as you make your way through remote wilderness areas to small pockets of settlements. Your reward will be a glimpse at a fascinating Southern culture and some of the finest natural landscapes that America offers.

Besides these major subregions, some other important regions of the South for the traveler to know and explore are the Bluegrass country of northern Kentucky, which is known for its fertile grasses that support horse grazing and a very active horse racing and breeding community; the Mississippi Delta region between the Yazoo and Mississippi rivers, with its rich soil and thriving cities of Memphis, Tennessee, and Vicksburg, Mississippi; the Outer Banks, which are a narrow chain of islands off the North Carolina coast; and the Florida Keys, a string of lovely coral islands that extend into the Gulf of Mexico.

Natural Features to Explore

Lovers of geology and natural history will not be disappointed in the South. The region contains many areas of exceptional beauty or unusual landscapes. During your travels, you can visit pristine lakes that are home to enormous gatherings of wildfowl, as well as alligators and crocodiles; marshy swamps and bayous where the trees are draped with Spanish moss; mountains that vividly display the vast array of hardwood trees that are indigenous to America; and canyons, caves, and rock features that have been carved for eons by wind and water. If you are a lover of natural history, be sure to include some of the following destinations, described from north to south, in your travel plans.

Virginia's Natural Bridge. In Virginia's Blue Ridge Mountains, about a day's ride due west of Richmond, is this magnificent natural arch that nature has hewn from solid rock. Standing 215 feet (65.5m) tall, with an opening that is 90 feet (27m) wide, the bridge is an awe-inspiring spectacle. Jefferson bought the property from the British Crown in 1774, shortly before he wrote the Declaration of Independence; careful visitors will find a young George Washington's initials carved on a rock wall from when he surveyed the region in 1750. You will likely meet groups of European tourists at the bridge, because along with Niagara Falls it is the most visited natural site in the nation. The Forest Inn, built in 1833 after Jefferson's heirs sold the property, is a comfortable lodging.

Great Dismal Swamp. On the eastern border of Virginia and North Carolina, just south of Norfolk, Virginia, this 30-mile-long (48km) swamp of some 200,000

Pictured here is Virginia's Natural Bridge, one of the state's many geological wonders.

acres (80,937 hectares) is part of a complex of swamplands along Albemarle and Pamlico sounds that cover nearly 2 million acres (809,371 hectares). One traveler described the swamp as "a vast quagmire, the soil being entirely composed of decayed vegetable fibre, saturated and surcharged with water [and] quaking on the surface to the tread of a man."[10] Inside are forests of hardwoods, which are logged by teams of slaves who pull up submerged stumps with pikes or hooks. Much of the timber is cut into shingles and shipped north to Philadelphia and Boston.

Great Smoky Mountains. This mountainous region of more than a half-million acres (202,342 hectares) on the Tennessee–North Carolina border is one of the greatest hardwood forests in the nation. Here you will find majestic stands of chestnut, oak, yellow birch, and American beech, and sugar maple trees whose leaves turn vibrant colors of red and gold in the autumn. Large populations of bear and deer roam the area, as well as bison, river otters, and red and gray wolves. Adventurers might wish to climb Clingmans Dome, at 6,643 feet (2,025m) the highest peak in the state of Tennessee.

Okefenokee Swamp. In the southeastern corner of Georgia, where Georgia meets northern Florida, this 700-acre (283 hectares) swamp is the largest in North America. Travelers who navigate its waters via canoe or flatboat will find a fascinating environment that is rich in native wildlife and indigenous plants. Look for forests packed with blackgum, bay, and cyprus trees, and floating mats of peat that are known as tree islands for their profusion of trees. Of the hundreds of species of birds and animals, try to spot blue herons, white ibises, and blue-winged teals, and keep an eye out for large mammals that include deer, black bear, and bobcats.

Florida Everglades. The largest subtropical wilderness in the United States at over 1.5 million acres (607,028 hectares), this vast region of south Florida is a nearly impenetrable jungle of mangrove channels, swamps, and forest. Waterfowl abound here, as do more dangerous creatures, such as crocodiles, alligators, and venomous snakes. Fishing opportunities are abundant, and if you are very lucky, you might spot a manatee surfacing when you are on the water.

To reach the Everglades, make your way south from St. Augustine on a three-to-five day ride to Lake Okeechobee, and then buy or make a boat to reach the southern edge of the lake. From there, hire a native Seminole guide to assist you in exploring this fascinating region.

Louisiana Bayou. West of New Orleans and extending for hundreds of miles is the

An alligator basks on a log in a cypress swamp in Louisiana. Alligators and other exotic creatures are common sights in the swamps and bayous of the South.

great Louisiana Bayou, which is created by the confluence of the Mississippi River and the Gulf of Mexico, as well as the vast drainage basin of the Atchafalaya River. Here you will find mysterious channels of water, such as the Bayou Teche, cutting through great groves of cypress trees and Spanish moss, as well as a lively culture of the Creoles and Acadians (known locally as Cajuns) who have settled the area. Look for wildlife that includes alligators, nutria, armadillos, opossum, raccoon, and mink: If you do not see them in the wild, they may very well turn up on the dinner tables of the locals, whose native cuisine is bold and distinctive.

An anonymous English writer whose articles appeared in a recent issue of *Edinburgh Magazine* had these first impressions of the bayou:

The character of the vegetation is totally different from anything to which we are accustomed; the beautiful live oak fans with its quivering leaves the glassy surface of the bayous; the waving cypress, here the most valuable tree of the forest, fringes its margin; the sweet gum and common oak, smothered in creepers and Spanish moss . . . the yellow hickory and fan-leaved palmetto and graceful cane conceal the sturdy trunks of the larger trees, which, meeting overhead, form an almost impenetrable shade as we

glide beneath them; alligators in numbers bask on the banks like stranded logs; bright plumaged birds glance among the branches, and vie in their plumage with bright-coloured flowers.[11]

The Southern Climate: Mild Winters, Hot Summers

"Nowhere in the world could a man, with a sound body and a quiet conscience, live more pleasantly, at least as a guest, it seems to me, than here where I am," wrote Frederick Law Olmsted, the noted New York writer and landscape designer, who traveled to Georgia in February 1853. "Everything encourages cheerfulness, and invites to healthful life."[12]

Like many travelers, Olmsted was thrilled to see green oranges growing on trees, the blooming camellias, the chirping sparrows and cooing doves, but mostly, he was delighted by the South's weather. More and more Northerners are discovering that they can escape the ice and snow of a cold, Northern winter

Get Away from the Heat as Southerners Do

Southerners know that escaping the heat of summer can be crucial to survival, and that is why you will find cities like Mobile and New Orleans nearly evacuated during July and August. It is best to plan your travels to avoid the hottest places in the South during the summer months. Instead, do what the Southerners do and visit the mountains or a cool lake during the summer. The planters of Louisiana can usually be found summering at Lake Pontchartrain outside of New Orleans, where many well-heeled businessmen own cottages and beautifully decorated vacation homes. Charleston and Savannah society generally packs up the family and summers in western Virginia's mineral springs communities. Located high up in the mountains, the springs at Hot, Warm, Sweet, Red Sulphur, and White Sulphur are centers of Southern society where families return every summer to socialize and court.

for the mild climate of the South, and as Olmsted discovered, the public houses from Virginia to Florida are packed with visitors during the winter months.

Those hailing from the North may be shocked to learn that one can often dispense with one's overcoat, even in the middle of February, in much of the South, and the flannels and furs with which one must wrap oneself during a Northern winter can be left behind on a visit to the South. The normal high temperature on an Alabama day in January is a balmy 61 degrees (16 degrees Celsius); the average low is just 40 degrees (4.4 degrees Celsius). The temperatures are similar in Georgia, Louisiana, Mississippi, South Carolina, and northern Florida. The states of Virginia, North Carolina, and Tennessee tend to be cooler in the winter, with average high temperatures of 50 degrees (10 degrees Celsius) and lows of around 30 (-1 degrees Celsius).

During the summer months, the South heats up. Louisiana temperatures reach an average high of 91 degrees (33 degrees Celsius) in July and August, and low temperatures average 74 degrees (23 degrees Celsius). Every state in the Deep South has seen record high temperatures of over 100 degrees (38 degrees Celsius). Combined with high humidity, the Southern states can be exceedingly hot and uncomfortable during the height of the summer. As a German visitor, Johann Schoepf, remarked, "Carolina is in the spring a paradise, in the summer a hell, and in the autumn a hospital."[13]

Diseases and Natural Disasters

The South's mild winter temperatures are considered to be conducive to good health, and many people come to be rejuvenated and regain their strength and health. "I had sought the South . . . as to find a healing balm in its mild and healthy climate for my injured health,"[14] writes A. De Puy Van Buren, a schoolteacher from Michigan who recently relocated to Yazoo County, Mississippi. Generally, the climate and the vigorous outdoor activities that are available throughout the year in the South are excellent for restoring one's health.

The hot, humid Southern summer, however, is frequently accompanied by severe outbreaks of disease, including yellow fever, cholera, and dysentery. The danger can be significant: Only a few years ago, the town of Alexandria, Louisiana, lost nearly half of its summer population to an outbreak of yellow fever. Nearly 700 of the town's residents left to escape the summer heat, but of the 300 who remained, 120 died. New Orleans also witnesses severe outbreaks of yellow fever: Newspaper accounts grimly reported death tolls of as many as 300 people a day from an outbreak in 1853, and planters and merchants fled the city with their families and slaves to avoid contagion. Quarantine appears to be the only way to contain an outbreak; the application of leeches may draw poisons from the blood if treatment is sought early.

The South can also be besieged by floods that swell the rivers and make

Victims of yellow fever in New Orleans writhe in pain as an onlooker flees. Visitors should be mindful that outbreaks of the disease are common in the summertime.

them overflow, wiping out crops, homes, and whole towns. For example, Mississippi planter Wade Hampton, who owns the Wild Woods Plantation and many other large concerns, recently had to evacuate his home to escape rising waters. As he wrote to his sister:

We are in great danger from the river, which is higher than it has ever been. . . . Many of the levees are broken and Steels Bayou is rising very rapidly. I am very much afraid that we shall all be overflowed, and I must wait a little while to see what will be the result. If the river does not fall very soon, we shall have the most disastrous freshet ever known in this valley.[15]

On the Atlantic Coast, hurricanes can wreak havoc, particularly during the month of September. Residents of coastal cities like Charleston and Savannah watch carefully for the signs of a storm, and try to secure their homes and families from danger. In Texas, Kentucky, and Tennessee, tornadoes in the spring and early summer months can wipe out whole towns and hundreds of acres of crops.

Though not generally advertised, famines are, unfortunately, a recurring fact of life in the South, despite the region's long growing season and ability to

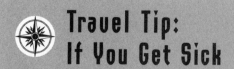

Travel Tip: If You Get Sick

Falling ill is sometimes an unavoidable risk of travel. Rest assured, if you happen to come down ill during a hosted visit to a plantation home, that Southern hospitality includes sheltering the sick. Rest is generally the best treatment, but if your condition dictates more advanced care, your hosts will summon a doctor who can bleed you, cup your temples, or administer laudanum for pain.

produce corn, soybeans, and other food crops. In 1837, farmers and plantation owners were forced to sell their slaves in order to buy food to fend off outright starvation. Other slaves were sent from the fields to fish and hunt for food until the crisis passed, because their masters could no longer feed them. In the last five years alone, famines have been reported in parts of northern Alabama, Georgia, and western South Carolina. Many people are without corn, and without means to procure any. Travelers are turned away from formerly hospitable homes because of the lack of available food, and horses and mules have been turned out into the woods to forage or starve. Travelers are thus advised to prepare for the possibility of food shortages by packing basic provisions—biscuits, dried meats, and the like—and verifying that food supplies are adequate at their destinations.

Chapter 3

Getting to the South

The South offers the most modern amenities for travelers, from lavishly appointed steamships that ply the mighty waters of the Mississippi and the South's other rivers, to locomotives, stagecoaches, and horse-drawn carriages that reach the region's largest cities and towns. To get to smaller villages or plantations, travelers must buy or rent a horse, which they may attempt to sell at the completion of their journey.

Travelers who wish to see large parts of the South will find themselves utilizing every method of transportation. When Olmsted set forth from Washington, D.C., in 1853 on a three-month tour of the South, he utilized  steamboats, trains, and stagecoaches to visit much of eastern Virginia, the Carolinas, Georgia, and Alabama, with only occasional uses of rented horses. Subsequent journeys through Texas and the vast cotton plantations of Louisiana and Mississippi required the purchase of horses, a pack mule, and a large array of supplies for an extended saddle trip. To truly explore the South, plan your journey carefully and employ a variety of transportation options.

Getting There by Train

One of the great advances of this decade is the expansion of the railroad system throughout the South. The 1850s started out with nine thousand miles of tracks in place throughout the United States, and the number has increased annually. In Georgia alone, there are now more than 1,200 miles (1,931km) of track. Most of the South's major cities can be reached by rail. You may be astonished by the speed at which you can travel, since trains move along at a speed of up to 25 miles per hour (40kph), which is twice as fast as a stagecoach. Many trains are capable of going even faster, but purposefully run slower because of the heavy toll that the rails and rail beds take. Broken tracks are common and cause derailments and the cancellation of service.

A good place to start for your railroad trip into the South is Baltimore, where the Baltimore and Ohio Railroad was the first passenger railroad in the country when it opened on July 4, 1828. Back then, the tracks went only 1.5 miles (2.4km), the cars were pulled by horses, and passengers rode along for the sheer novelty of the journey. "We only repeat the general sentiment when we say, it is the most delightful of all kinds of traveling,"[16] wrote a reporter for the *Baltimore Gazette*. Charleston, South Carolina, was the site of the nation's first steam locomotive, the "Best Friend of Charleston," when it debuted on Christmas Day 1830. Three years later, the South Carolina Railroad boasted the world's longest service when it completed tracks from Charleston to Hamburg, South Carolina, 136 miles (219km) away. The journey between the two cities took eleven and a half hours (an average of nearly 12 miles

Powerful locomotives allow travelers to journey throughout the South at terrific speeds. Today's trains are capable of reaching speeds of up to twenty-five miles per hour.

(19kph) per hour and cost $6.75 each way.

Now, the B&O travels hundreds of miles due west to the town of Wheeling, Ohio, where passengers can disembark and catch a steamboat south on the Ohio River into Kentucky and points south, or continue their journey into the South via stagecoach. There are dozens of regional train companies. In Georgia, the Savannah and Macon line, established in 1834, crosses the entirety of Georgia in twenty-four hours at a brisk pace of 15 to 20 miles (24 to 32kph) per hour. The line is one of the most profitable railroads in the United States, with annual receipts of more than $1 million.

Travel Tip: The Drawbacks of Train Travel

Passengers sometimes complain about the great noise that a locomotive makes, and some people object to being constantly showered by ashes and glowing, hot cinders from the coal-burner's great smokestacks. Baggage handlers are sometimes referred to as baggage smashers for the way that they treat luggage. Some trains keep strict schedules, and others may be hours or even days late. Do not trust porters or conductors to tell you truthfully when the train will leave; they are frequently misinformed. Be sure to stay within hearing distance of the train station to make sure that you are not left behind.

Train fares are calculated by the mile and can range from two-and-three-quarters to more than four cents per mile. This buys you a seat—sometimes on a plain, wooden bench; sometimes upholstered—in a public car. Most trains combine first-class passenger cars with freight cars that are loaded with bales of cotton heading to market, as well as slaves who are being "sold south" to the cotton plantations of the Deep South that are continually in need of new laborers. Depending on the temperature outside and the time of day, try to have the porter seat you in a desirable proximity to the car's furnace, which is stoked with wood throughout the journey by a steward. Sit too close and you may suffocate from the heat and smoke that the furnace produces; too far away and you will catch a chill from the drafts that stream through the cars.

Getting There by Boat

Traveling into the Deep South by boat down a mighty river may take quite a bit longer than other means of transportation (about four times slower than a train and only half as fast as carriage travel), but many travelers believe the comforts of the trip far outweigh the loss in speed. Steamboats can carry you along the Gulf of Mexico from Mobile to New Orleans; down the Potomac River from Washington, D.C., to Richmond, Virginia (fare: $2); up the Red River into the heart of Louisiana, or north through Tennessee and Kentucky on the Ohio and Mississippi rivers. The

Paddleboat steamers travel down the mighty Mississippi River in an engraving by Currier and Ives.

fares are similar to train travel, in the range of two-to-four cents per mile.

On the Mississippi River, you can catch any number of large, handsome paddleboat steamers that cruise leisurely down the great river all the way to the thriving city of New Orleans. These ships are beautifully decorated and come equipped with traveling theatrical troupes and entertainers who perform everything from Shakespearean plays to minstrel shows. Consider this description in *Hunt's Magazine* of a steamboat named *The Empire State*, a lavishly appointed ship that plies the waters of the great river:

The word boat gives a very imperfect idea of this floating palace, which accommodates . . . from five to six hundred American citizens and others, of all classes, in a style of splendor that Cleopatra herself might envy. . . . I followed a crowd of five hundred up a handsome staircase, through splendidly furnished saloons covered with carpet of velvet pile, to the upper deck. Tea being served, we all adjourned to the gentlemen's cabin. . . . At the entrance we were met by tall, swarthy figures, clothed in white linen of unspotted purity, who conducted us to our seats. There were three tables, the entire length of the room covered with everything that was beautiful.[17]

Try to secure a private cabin in advance by making a reservation with the clerk of the ship. If you fail to secure a berth, the ship's staff may hang sleeping cots, which are rows of canvas sheets that are barely long and wide enough for a man, in the dining room. The cots ac-

Reading Material for Your Trip

Southern newspapers, with their fiery editorials and local color, are a fine way to learn more about the South. Pick them up at every major city. The *Southern Literary Messenger* has seen a slight decline since Edgar Allen Poe, a one-time editor and frequent contributor, passed away in 1849, but it remains the preeminent literary magazine in the South. One of the *Messenger*'s best writers and illustrators, David Hunter Strother, has begun placing his work in *Harper's New Monthly Magazine*, which is enjoyed as much in the South as in the rest of the country. You will find that many Southern plantation owners enjoy the adventurous, historical novels of Sir Walter Scott, but the book in nearly every traveler's bag this season is Harriett Beecher Stowe's novel, *Uncle Tom's Cabin*, which combines the author's abolitionist views with a tender story about a family of slaves. It sold three hundred thousand copies in 1852 when it was first published, and a million copies a year later.

Uncle Tom's Cabin *is recommended reading for any visitor to the South.*

commodate dozens of travelers in a tight, cramped space; try to get one close to the door in order to get adequate ventilation. You might try to find a quiet place to sleep on the freight levels of the ship, but frequently the bales of cotton and boxes of merchandise are occupied by groups of slaves, as well as travelers who cannot afford first-class passage. If you cannot sleep and want to try your luck at gambling, you can always find a card game in progress somewhere on the boat. Professional gamblers earn their living by playing against passengers, and the most successful gamblers employ "strikers," or men who scout the passengers and try to entice those with money to join the game.

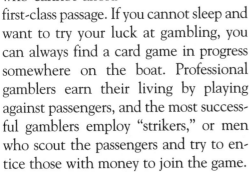

Steamship travel is slow in part because most ships will stop at nearly every bend in the river to deliver goods to a village or plantation, or to load bales of cotton or merchandise to be carried downriver. As Olmsted reported from the steamboat *Fashion* on a voyage in Alabama between Montgomery and Mobile, "There are two hundred landings on the Alabama River, and three hundred on the Bigby . . . at which the boats advertise to call, if required, for passengers or freight. This, of course, makes the passage exceedingly tedious."[18] Passengers in many cases can hail a passing ship from the shore and expect to have it interrupt its journey in order to pick them up. Frequent stops are made for "wooding" the boat, or filling it up with fresh wood for the firebox, and slaves are usually on hand to leap off the boat to cut and load fresh wood during the journey.

Although generally safe, steamboats can also catch fire or run aground and break up, endangering all passengers and cargo. We recently received word that the steamboat *Unicorn* was completely destroyed by fire on the Yazoo River in Mississippi just two weeks before Christmas. There was no word of injuries, but one plantation owner lost all fifty-five bales of her cotton on the ship. "I am in hops you had good inshurrans on it,"[19] wrote her overseer.

Alternatives to the Steamboat

Another way to get downriver is to buy an ark, also known as a broadhorn, scow, or Kentucky flatboat, at a way station along the Ohio or Mississippi rivers. This simple craft, with a crude shelter in the center for passengers and cargo, is a flat raft that drifts on the rivers' currents. It costs about seventy-five dollars and accommodates three or four families, who then endeavor to sell the craft downriver for what they paid for it.

The Plantation South

To travel from the ports of New York or Boston to the Southern cities of Savannah or Charleston, try to arrange passage on a schooner or a clipper ship, which are very fast ocean-going sailing vessels that typically carry great quantities of cargo, but can also accommodate a small number of passengers. Beware of traveling during the hurricane season of August and September, when many ships are lost to ferocious storms.

Clipper ship.

Getting There by Road

Travelers on horseback or in carriages can enter the South via a track that has been called America's first great highway. The Great Philadelphia Wagon Road first enters the South in Maryland, just south of Gettysburg, Pennsylvania, and then winds its way south through Virginia and North Carolina all the way into the woods of South Carolina. The Wilderness Road was the trail blazed by

Travelers unable to afford steamboat passage find Kentucky flatboats like this one to be an attractive alternative.

Daniel Boone in 1775 that allows movement between Tennessee through the Cumberland Gap to Kentucky. Bear in mind that tolls have been imposed on this main road since 1797. In Louisiana, the Natchez Trace is a former Indian trail that was once traveled by de Soto and French explorers. This main thoroughfare, connecting Natchez and Louisiana to eastern Tennessee and the town of Nashville, is a favorite route for flatboatmen who sell their goods and boats in New Orleans.

Travelers seeking to leave the beaten path can strike out on all manner of pikes, paths, and "corduroy roads." These are primitive roads built of logs and saplings that have been laid side by side and covered roughly with dirt and mud. The less adventurous are advised to steer clear.

Southern governments are actively involved in road-building and road-improvement projects, largely to help farmers and merchants deliver their products to markets more quickly. In the 1850s, North Carolina in particular has been at the forefront of building "plank roads," which are thoroughfares constructed of thick planks of wood, 8 to 15 feet (2.5 to 4.6m) wide, with frequent turnouts for slower-moving carts to give way. The plank roads are financed by tolls, with an individual rider on horseback charged one-half cent per mile, and a two-horse team or wagon charged two cents per mile. The longest plank road in history, at 129 miles (208km), was just opened in 1854 from Fayetteville to Bethania by way of High Point.

Stagecoach companies have scheduled service between major towns, with their runs designed to coincide with

Do Not Forget Your Knife and Pistols

A word about safety: Although the South is generally hospitable and safe, the alert traveler must always be prepared for the occasional stagecoach robbery or mugging by unsavory characters, many of whom linger along roads and thoroughfares to waylay unprepared travelers. Many people protect themselves by carrying either a Bowie knife, that long, deadly blade of steel popularized by Jim Bowie, or its Southern equivalent, the Arkansas toothpick. You may also wish to carry your brace of dueling pistols, because Southern men value their honor highly and are known to avenge any perceived insult with a duel. For complete rules about dueling conduct, consult Governor John Lyde Wilson of South Carolina's sixteen-page pamphlet on the subject.

Dueling pistols

railroad arrivals and departures. Fares run from one to two dollars depending on the length of travel. There are also a number of carriage manufacturers who sell gigs, sulkeys, barouches, and buggies to travelers who wish to travel privately.

If you are planning to stay within a specific region, you can rent a fine riding horse for two dollars a day, but you must return the horse to its owner. Otherwise, you can buy a horse and tack and sell them at the end of your journey.

Horse and buggy is yet another mode of travel available to visitors. Travelers should be extremely wary, however, of the deplorable conditions of many Southern roads.

Keep in mind that traveling via roads is not always easy. There is no signage; roads can quickly peter out into confusing paths or muddy tracks; and it can be very difficult to get clear directions from locals. Roads get washed out due to heavy rains and mud, and it is not uncommon for even the finest carriages to sink up to their hubs in mud, forcing all passengers to disembark and help to dig their coach out. The quality of the roads even affects the social life in the South. "The people live so far apart and the roads are so abominably bad that it is out of the question to have evening parties," wrote one traveler in Virginia. "It would frighten a country Virginian half to death to be out till nine o'clock in the evening."[20]

Rutted roads, tired horses, and drunk stagecoach drivers account for frequent mishaps. Passengers should expect and be mentally prepared for at least one incident of the stagecoach turning over during a journey. An English traveler once described his carriage ride as being "tossed about like a few potatoes in a wheelbarrow. Our knees, elbows, and heads required too much care for their protection to allow us leisure to look out of windows."[21]

Service and courtesy on board a stagecoach can be, at best, minimal. On a trip to Gaston, North Carolina, Olmsted was left behind by a stagecoach that loaded his luggage and then departed early. He walked several miles through a wood to intercept the coach, was unceremoniously bumped and jostled and

Travel Tip: How Long Will It Take?

It can be difficult to estimate the amount of time you will need when traveling through the South. One young man who recently moved from Battle Creek, Michigan, to Yazoo County, Mississippi—a distance of 855 miles (1,376km)—reported that the journey took him twelve full days. The speed of your trip will vary depending on if you can utilize railroads and riverboats, which keep regular schedules, or if much of your journey depends on stagecoach and saddle transfers. If you must depend heavily on the latter, expect to travel no more than 20 to 30 miles (32 to 48km) per day, and expect frequent delays.

then overturned on a journey of 14 miles (22.5km) that took four hours, and then was left with his fellow passengers and their baggage in the dark on a bluff overlooking a riverbank to wait for a ferry that never came. The passengers found a railroad bridge upriver to cross, and then hired a private boat to return for their baggage. On another journey, the driver could not get his exhausted, mistreated horses to move; he beat them viciously and then left on one to ride ahead to secure new horses, leaving his passengers behind. Olmsted left the stagecoach and walked 10 miles (16km) to the next way station, beating his fellow passengers by several hours.

The stagecoach is an extremely convenient way to travel between towns and cities not connected by railroad lines. Schedules are unreliable, however, and accidents are common.

What to Pack

For the trip to the South, you will want simple, sturdy clothing that can withstand the rigors of travel, including dust, mud, cinders that rain down from locomotive smokestacks, rain, and the tobacco expectorations of your fellow travelers, with whom you will be in close quarters for days on end. Keep in mind that porters are not always available, and you may be required to carry your belongings for several miles at a time.

Women should not forget to pack their most elegant ball gowns, petticoats, hats, and crinolines, in case they have the opportunity to attend a Plantation Ball. Men will want to bring along suits, their best boots and albert (the short chain that connects a watch fob to a buttonhole), and a bang-up, or stylish overcoat. Keep in mind that the South's major cities have plenty of talented seamstresses and shops that import the latest fashions from as far away as New

York and Paris, and you can always supplement your traveling wardrobe with new purchases.

If you are planning an extended trip on horseback through the South's more rural areas, you will need to equip yourself with all of the necessities of an extended camping trip, including blankets, overcoats, guns, a tent, medicines and supplies, emergency rations, lanterns and candles, matches, and reading material.

Budgeting Your Trip

How much will your trip through the South cost? A precise figure is hard to say. Ask yourself before your trip if you plan to seek comfortable lodgings every night, or if you are willing to camp out under the stars. Do you have contacts or introductions to secure invitations from planters, or are you hoping to be invited for extended stays with strangers whom you meet? Keep in mind that many travelers have been disappointed to learn that all plantation homes do not throw open their doors free of charge to any and all visitors. Many expect payment for room and board. Your transportation costs will also vary depending on how far into the South you wish to travel, and if you will utilize more expensive trains and steamboats, rather than flatboats and stagecoaches.

Proper Manners on a Stagecoach

An experienced traveler offers this good advice for surviving your trip on a stagecoach with maximum comfort and courtesy toward other guests:

The best seat inside a stagecoach is the one next to the driver. You will have to ride with [your] back to the horses, which with some people, produces an illness not unlike sea sickness, but in a long journey this will wear off, and you will get more rest. . . . Bathe your feet before starting in cold weather, and wear loose overshoes and gloves two to three sizes too large. When the driver asks you to get off and walk, do it without grumbling. . . . If a team runs away, sit still and take your chances; if you jump, nine times out of ten you will be hurt. . . . Don't swear, nor lop over on your neighbor when sleeping. . . . Never attempt to fire a gun or pistol while on the road; it may frighten the team and the careless handling and cocking of the weapon makes nervous people nervous. Don't discuss politics or religion, nor point out places on the road where horrible murders have been committed, if delicate women are among the passengers.

The Plantation South

As a general rule, private citizens who take in travelers typically request a dollar and a quarter for a night's lodging and two meals, which is similar to hotel rates, and other meals on the road range from fifty cents to a dollar. If you are invited to stay at a large, prosperous plantation, you can expect free food and lodging for the duration of your visit, but such invitations are rare.

Olmsted's recent journey illustrates well the cost of travel these days. For his first journey of three months through Virginia, the Carolinas, Georgia, Alabama, and Mississippi, he reported that he was spending approximately two dollars a day outside of transportation costs, and he expected the entire journey to cost about three hundred dollars.

Chapter 4

Visiting Plantations

At the very heart of the South's prosperity and society, not to mention a growing legend of Southern hospitality and largesse, lies the plantation. A Southern plantation is both a home and a business, typically owned by a single person or family of illustrious name. It usually comprises the following: hundreds or thousands of acres of arable land being cultivated with cash  crops and food crops; resident quarters that are usually a striking mansion or architecturally distinctive home surrounded by attractive landscaping and gardens; houses for the slaves who work the land and serve the family; and shops and outbuildings that serve the operations of the plantation.

What distinguishes a plantation from a large farm is that a plantation owns at least twenty slaves. It is generally recognized in today's South that a truly wealthy plantation employs fifty or more slaves. The number of slaves needed is determined by the amount of land that is cultivated; hence the need for more slaves on a plantation that has larger arable lands. The number of such large planters is very small. The latest census shows that of 1.25 million white families, only 347,000, or a little more than a quarter, own any slaves at all. Only 8,000 persons own fifty or more slaves, and of these, only 1,800 own one hundred or more slaves.

How much land can a plantation owner acquire and manage? That

The typical Southern plantation boasts an impressive number of slaves. In this photograph, elegantly dressed slaves wait to greet visitors to a plantation in South Carolina.

question is constantly being tested by today's aggressive owners, with numbers of acres and slaves reaching ever higher. Consider Wade Hampton III of Mississippi, who through a combination of inheritance and purchases, now owns the Wild Woods Plantation of 835 acres (338 hectares); Bayou Place with 2,729 acres (1,104 hectares); Otterbourne at 1,354 acres (548 hectares); Walnut Ridge at 2,529 acres (1,023 hectares); and Bear Gardens at 2,962 acres (1,199 hectares).

The combined 10,409 acres (4,212 hectares) of land are worked by nine hundred slaves, producing enormous profits every year for Mr. Hampton.

Five Must-See Plantations

There are thousands of plantations scattered throughout the South. Some are run by the owner-planters in residence; others are managed by overseers who are hired by absentee owners to run the business of the plantation. Each plantation is distinctive in its own way, but the following five are exceptional. If your travels take you within a day's ride of any of these plantations, make a point to stop and visit them.

Monticello (near Charlottesville, Virginia). Jefferson's Virginia estate has seen some drastic changes since his death nearly thirty years ago, but Monticello continues to be among the most magnificent dwellings in America. Built in a Roman neoclassical style, it has forty-three rooms, 11,000 square feet (1,022 sq. m), and an entrance hall with 18.5-foot (5.6m) ceilings. The library houses the finest private collection of books in the country, as well as many rare artifacts from the West that were sent to Jefferson from the Lewis and Clark Expedition. Many of Jefferson's furnishings, farm equipment, and slaves were sold in 1827 to pay his debts, and the lands surrounding Monticello dwindled from more than 5,000 acres (2,023 hectares) to 522 (211 hectares). Nevertheless, the present home of naval officer Uriah P. Levy, an admirer of Jefferson and the third owner of Monticello, continues to be the jewel of Virginia plantations.

Madewood (Between Baton Rouge and New Orleans, Louisiana). This brandnew estate of sugar planter Thomas Pugh on the River Road, which packs 350 mansions into a 100-mile (161km) stretch of some of the most fertile land in the Louisiana Delta, has already been called the "Queen of the Bayou" since its completion in 1854. Eight years in the making, it was fashioned from six hundred thousand bricks formed from local clay, and features 11,000 square feet (1,022 sq. m) of living space that includes a lovely ballroom with 16-foot (5m) ceilings. After dinner in a candlelit dining room that features a long, custom-made oak table, repair to an English wing chair in the library or spend the evening in the

Travel Tip: Carry Letters of Introduction

The best way to secure an invitation to a plantation is by carrying letters of introduction. Before embarking on your trip, ask your friends and business associates if they have any connections to Southern planters or businessmen, and have your contacts write a letter of introduction that you can present upon arrival in the South. If you do not have any mutual acquaintances, ask a prominent businessman or politician in your community to provide you with a letter of reference. This letter should state who you are, your profession, and your good standing in your community. Present it at places in the South where you wish to stay and it will literally open doors for you.

Monticello, near Charlottesville, Virginia, remains one of the South's finest plantation houses, although its Roman neoclassical architecture is atypical.

music room admiring original art by European masters and the music from an eighteenth-century Hiller organ.

Shirley Plantation (18 miles (29km) southeast of Richmond, Virginia). The oldest plantation in Virginia, dating back to 1613, is also the oldest family-owned business in the country since Edward Hill I began to cultivate the plantation in 1638. The handsome brick mansion at the centerpiece of the plantation has hosted statesmen who include Washington, Jefferson, and the Marquis de Lafayette. Army General Robert E. Lee spent his childhood studying here; his mother, Anne Hill Carter, was born at Shirley and was married to "Light-Horse" Harry Lee in the mansion's parlor in 1793. Be sure to linger over the hand-carved woodwork and the "flying" staircase that ascends three stories without visible supports. Outbuildings feature a distinctive Queen Anne design.

 # A Visit to Shirley Plantation

The grandeur and wealth of a Southern plantation is summed up in a letter home by twenty-two-year-old Henry Barnard of Hartford, Connecticut, after he spent a night at Virginia's Shirley Plantation in 1837:

> It consists of about 900 acres improved land of the first quality, and 100 slaves and yields an income of nearly 10,000 dollars. He has this year a field of wheat, of only 320 acres, and raises for market about 300 barrels of corn. He keeps 20 horses. With such an income you may imagine his splendid hospitality. His service is all of silver, and you drink your porter out of silver goblets. The table at dinner is always furnished with the finest Virginia ham, and saddle of mutton—turkey, then cava back duck—beef—oysters, etc, etc, etc—the finest celery—then comes the sparkling champagne—after that the dessert, plum pudding—tarts—ice cream—peaches preserved in Brandy etc, etc—then the table is cleared, and on comes the figs, almonds and raisins, and the richest Madeira, the best Port and the softest Malmsey wine I ever tasted.

Visitors should not overlook Shirley Plantation near Richmond, Virginia, the oldest plantation in the state.

The Plantation South

Hampton Plantation (St. Simons Island, Georgia). This thriving plantation owned by the dashing Pierce Meese Butler has made a fortune out of cultivating long-staple Sea Island cotton. One plantation guest was Aaron Burr, the duelist who killed Alexander Hamilton. Burr wrote of Hampton's "cream and butter; turkeys, fowls, kids, pigs, geese and mutton: fish, of course, in abundance. Of figs, peaches, and melons there are yet a few. Oranges and pomegranates just beginning to be eatable."[22] Butler's wife, and the mistress of Hampton, is the English actress Fanny Kemble, a star of the London stage who came to America and is known for her sharp wit and keen observations about the lives and habits of Southerners.

Nottoway Plantation (South of Baton Rouge, Louisiana, on the Mississippi River). The rich sugar fields owned by John Hampden Randolph, a transplanted Virginian, fuel a lifestyle of almost unimaginable wealth. The mansion has fifty

The heart of the Southern plantation is the manor house. This one, at Nottoway Plantation near Baton Rouge, Louisiana, is one of the largest and finest examples.

rooms that are lavishly decorated with bronze and crystal chandeliers, marble mantels, and intricate plaster moldings. The magnificent ballroom is a dazzling white from the enameled floor to the plastered ceiling. Randolph enjoys hunting, and employs tutors to teach literature, dancing, and music to his children. Gifts of books and newspapers are always welcome from visitors.

The Layout of the Plantation

The first thing a traveler might notice upon approaching a plantation is the outstanding landscaping that announces the mansion. The "Big House" generally occupies an elevated plot of land near the main road, with stately rows of oak trees leading up to its manicured lawns. Other trees planted for shade, visual appeal, and fragrance may include groves of magnolia, beech, boxwood, and elm. Magnolias in particular are distinctive to the South and provide "magnificent chandeliers of fragrance,"[23] as one visitor reported. Hedges are also used to great effect. The huge cotton plantations of the Deep South are frequently decorated with thick hedges of Cherokee rose and sweet briar and can grow to be 6 feet (2m) high and 10 feet (3m) deep.

The mansion is intentionally designed to be the grandest structure on the plantation. Generally built of two or three stories, it is nearly always fronted by long columns in Greek or Roman revival styles. Some travelers to the South have noted that even very modest homes have attempted to look more imposing by adding columns to their plain facades. Inside are long hallways and, in many cases, an imposing staircase that is the centerpiece of the home, with tall rooms whose long windows provide a cooling breeze during the hot summer months. During chilly winters, however, the same rooms can be drafty and cold, and a fireplace in each room is necessary to ward off the cold. The ground floors are generally reserved for public rooms, including a sitting room, pantry, and dining room, and the upper floors are occupied by bedrooms. The upstairs rooms will usually have an entrance to the balcony, and usually an outdoor staircase will lead to the upper balcony to provide quick and easy access.

Surrounding the mansion is a series of outbuildings necessary to daily life. These include a kitchen area, smokehouse, and cooking area, which not only remove the odors and noise of cooking from the main house, but protect the mansion from the dangers of kitchen fires. An icehouse may be nearby to store blocks of ice, and a dairy and well supply milk products and fresh water. Nearby will be the plantation's vegetable garden and orchards for supplying the food for the entire plantation.

Privies, or outhouses, will be discreetly located behind the house, usually near a grove of trees for the sake of privacy. There is no indoor plumbing, and

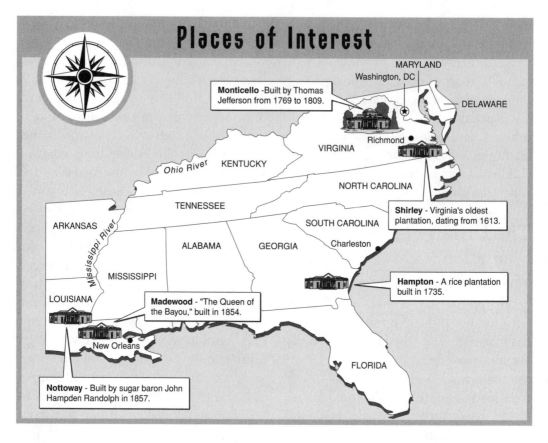

Places of Interest

MARYLAND

Washington, DC

Monticello -Built by Thomas Jefferson from 1769 to 1809.

DELAWARE

Richmond

VIRGINIA

Ohio River KENTUCKY

NORTH CAROLINA

TENNESSEE

Shirley - Virginia's oldest plantation, dating from 1613.

ARKANSAS

SOUTH CAROLINA

Mississippi River

ALABAMA GEORGIA Charleston

MISSISSIPPI

Hampton - A rice plantation built in 1735.

LOUISIANA

Madewood - "The Queen of the Bayou," built in 1854.

New Orleans

FLORIDA

Nottoway - Built by sugar baron John Hampden Randolph in 1857.

water is brought into the home in buckets and basins.

The plantation office will be close; this is where the plantation owner conducts his business. He will want to stay close to the manufacturing center of the plantation, where cotton is ginned or sugarcane is processed into brown sugar, molasses, or white sugar that is packaged in cones. Barns, stables, and storehouses will be at the edges of the properties, and a family burial ground with markers is maintained on the property.

Farther away will be the quarters of the slaves and overseers, as well as a hospital or sickhouse, storage sheds, and a burial ground for slaves. Surrounding the whole plantation, of course, are the acres and acres of land that are used to cultivate the cash crop that is sold to create the profits of the plantation.

Cotton Is King

Plantations can be enormously profitable when they are carefully managed, and when they are located in favorable growing zones. "Planters make more money than Presidents!" exclaimed young A. De Puy Van Buren upon visiting a Mississippi cotton plantation. "They are the whole year attending to it," he added. "One crop is scarcely secured ere enother is planted."[24]

The measure of a plantation's profitability is given in the amount of yield per acre, or yield per field hand, that the land can produce given an adequate amount of slave labor. As Olmsted reports:

I have been on plantations on the Mississippi, the Red River, and the Brazos bottoms, whereon I was assured that ten bales of cotton to each average prime field-hand had been raised. The soil was a perfect garden mould, well drained and guarded by levees against the floods; it was admirably tilled. . . . They

Slaves are hard at work picking cotton as an overseer on horseback monitors their work. For visitors traveling along rural roads in the South, scenes like this are very common.

Cotton and Tobacco: Enormous Profits for Enormous Work

The South's prosperity in the 1850s has been fueled by the huge profits that growers are reaping from the cultivation of cotton and tobacco. Both crops thrive in the hot, sunny summers and mild, frostless winters of the South, but they are anything but easy to cultivate. Cotton and tobacco require a huge amount of labor to plant, pick, and, in the case of tobacco, cure. Entire crops can be lost if planters, overseers, and work crews slacken in any phase of the growing season.

In North Carolina alone, tobacco production has nearly tripled from a yield of 12 million pounds (nearly 5.5 million kg) in 1850 to an expected 33 million pounds (13.6 million kg) by the end of the decade. The industry was revolutionized in 1852 when a slave of Abisha & Elisha Shade of Caswell County mistakenly cured a portion of tobacco leaves with charcoal, instead of the traditional wood.

The leaves turned bright yellow and the resultant "gold leaf" tobacco was highly sought after by worldwide markets. Tobacco growers must watch for blue mold, a fungus that appears with wet weather, and the crop must be harvested quickly if there is any danger of an early frost. Tobacco is also devastating to the soil in which it grows, depleting it rapidly of nutrients, and many tobacco patches are abandoned altogether after a few years, with new land cleared, plowed, and planted for subsequent yields.

Cotton grows freely, particularly in the Deep South, but it can easily be destroyed by grasses or weeds. Work crews spend long hours hoeing and tending to their cotton patches. When the distinctive white fibers burst from their pods, or bolls, the cotton is picked by hand. The bolls themselves are tough and razor-sharp, and many a field slave's hands are cut and bloodied by them.

had the best sort of gins and presses, so situated that from them cotton bales could be rolled in five minutes to steamboats, bound direct to the ports on the Gulf.[25]

At ten bales per hand, the profits of cotton can make plantation owners wealthy beyond description. Even at seven bales to the hand, the profits of cotton are enormous. In the prime cotton-growing areas of the South, many plantations produce seven bales to the hand for years in succession. Others pro-

duce seven bales occasionally. Rice sells for as much as seven cents a pound some years, yielding planters profits of hundreds of thousands of dollars. This is balanced by years when hurricanes and tornadoes can completely destroy a crop and leave the plantation with nothing.

In areas where the land is not as productive, plantation owners must go into debt to continue the operation of their business until a bumper crop is harvested. Family and slaves must still be fed and clothed, regardless of the value of the crop. Frequently, a planter must refinance his loan based on the need to purchase new equipment or labor, or to defray the burden of a bad crop. As Olmsted notes of planters of more modest circumstances, "He lives on, year to year, gaining a little on his debts but almost as often enlarging them."[26]

Sugar Plantations Going Strong

Sugar is another crop that produces handsome profits, but it is more difficult to find the right combination of land and labor to produce consistently good crops, and competition from the Caribbean islands is strong. The costs of starting a sugar plantation are also daunting. A refinery that can produce white loaf sugar as well as brown sugar and molasses costs roughly one hundred thousand dollars to build.

In 1849 there were 1,474 sugar estates in Louisiana that produced 236,547 hogsheads of sugar, but half of the production came from fewer than 200 estates. The best sugar land in the state produces 1,000 pounds (453kg) of

An overseer supervises slave children as they harvest sugarcane. Most of the large sugar plantations are located in Louisiana.

sugar per acre, but by contrast, growers in the West Indies are realizing yields of 3,000 to 6,000 pounds (1,361 to 2,722kg) per acre. An average yield for a plantation is 650 hogsheads of sugar, at anywhere from two to four cents a pound, and twelve hundred barrels of molasses at ten cents a gallon. The largest growers in Louisiana produce as much as 1 million pounds (453,592kg) of sugar per year, with resultant immense profits.

Plantation Food

The opulence of the plantation lifestyle is easy to see at mealtimes. Food is plentiful and abundant on most plantations. The Southern climate favors a wide variety of produce and a long growing season. Well-tended gardens supply lettuces and greens, as well as cucumbers, beans, squash, potatoes, and Southern specialties like turnips and okra. From the fields come corn, pumpkins, sweet potatoes, and rice. Orchards produce an array of fruits, including figs, apples, pears, quinces, and peaches, and growing wild are blackberries, plums, muscadines, and walnuts. Fish are abundant in rivers and creeks, and chickens and hogs supply the plantations with meat. The only foods that a visitor might miss are beef and mutton, which are scarce in the South due to insufficient grazing lands.

Southern planters dine like kings. Letitia M. Burwell, a tenth generation Virginia planter, writes the following about the foods that appear on her family table:

Time would fail me to dwell upon the incomparable rice waffles, and beat biscuits, and muffins, and laplands, and marguerites, and flannel cakes, and French rolls, and velvet rolls, and lady's fingers constantly brought by relays of small servants, during breakfast, hot and hotter from the kitchen. Then the tea-waiters handed at night, with the beef tongue, the sliced ham, the grated cheese, the cold turkey, the dried venison, the loaf bread buttered hot, the batter-cakes, the crackers, the quince marmalade, the wafers.[27]

Entire books have been written about Southern food specialties, but the following Southern favorites are particularly recommended:

spoonbread: Called "the top of the cornbread line," this is a fluffy, steaming cornmeal dish made with butter, milk, and eggs that, when carefully prepared, can practically serve as a dessert.

hominy: Corn that is processed with lye produces this snowy-white grain, which is sometimes referred to as "grits." "Ought always to be eaten with lumps of sweet fresh butter buried in it!, this is certainly one of the best things imaginable to begin the day liberally with,"[28] exclaimed one English visitor.

sweet potatoes: Dug up fresh and roasted in ashes, they are a staple of the Southern table at any meal. Sweet potato pie, made with brown sugar, eggs, cinnamon, and butter, is a Southern dessert specialty.

okra: A squashlike vegetable that grows in pods, okra is delicious when breaded and fried, and is often added to soups and stews, especially in combination with fresh tomatoes.

corn whiskey and bourbon: Generally served at the evening meal, the homemade liquors of the South range from fiery to mellow. Kentucky bourbons, which are filtered through charcoal and aged in oak barrels, are particularly appealing. "One Small drink would Stimulate the Whole Sistom," wrote one Kentuckian. ". . . It Brot out kind feelings of the Heart."[29]

bacon and collard greens: Stewed kale leaves picked fresh from Southern gardens, with bacon added for flavor, make a flavorful side dish.

mint juleps: Another popular libation, this delicious cocktail consists of brandy,

A Plantation Budget: What It Costs to Operate a Sugar Plantation in Louisiana for One Year

The following information was supplied to the secretary of the treasury in 1846 by sugar planters of St. Mary's Parish, Louisiana, and gives visitors an idea of the cost of running a typical large sugar plantation with one hundred slaves. We are indebted to Olmsted's *The Cotton Kingdom: A Traveller's Observations on Cotton and Slavery,* for these figures.

Overseer's salary	$1,500
Physician's attendance (by contract, $3 a head, of all ages)	300
Yearly repair to engine, copper work, resetting of sugar kettles, etc. at least	900
Engineer, during grinding season	200
Pork, 50 pounds per day—say, per annum, 90 hogsheads, at $12	1,080
Hoops	80
Clothing, two full suits per annum, shoes, caps, hats and 100 blankets, at least $15 per slave	1,500
Mules or horses, and cattle to replace, at least	500
Implements of husbandry, iron, nails, lime, etc., at least	1,000
Factor's commission, 2.5 per cent	500
	7,560

sugar, and sprigs of fresh mint leaves served in a tall glass filled with ice.

Plantation Entertainment and Activities

Plantation life revolves around the growing of crops, and proud plantation owners will want to show you their fields and machinery. Much of your daytime recreation may be spent on horseback with the owner, who will tour the plantation, make sure that work is being done correctly, and check with his overseer on the conditions of the work crew and the crop. Plantation owners are foremost very busy farmers and businessmen, and most of them enjoy discussing the business of the plantation with visitors.

Outdoor recreation might include hunting for squirrels, possum, and wild turkeys, or for bigger game like bear and

The quantity and quality of food served on Southern plantations is matched only by the warm hospitality some plantation families are known to extend to visitors.

deer. Southerners are also avid horsemen, particularly in Kentucky, where horses thrive on the bluegrass that grows wild, and a cottage industry in horse racing has begun among wealthy plantation owners. Fox hunts are favorite special events that involve tearing off across hill and dale on fast horses in pursuit of a cagey red fox.

Some plantations have tenpin bowling alleys on their grounds, with ladies participating with as much enthusiasm as the men, and many plantations engage in cockfights, with participants bringing their trained birds from miles around.

Music is very popular in plantation homes. Many have a music room equipped with a piano, and women and daughters are encouraged to learn to play the piano and sing. The music of Stephen Foster is popular, as family and guests alike sing "Oh! Susanna," "My Old Kentucky Home," and "Camptown Races." Another popular activity is cardplaying. Ladies in particular enjoy leisurely afternoons and evenings of playing whist and euchre.

At the end of the day, Southerners also love to gather on the porch, frequently with a mint julep to drink, and discuss the events of the day. Just sitting on the porch in a comfortable rocking

Merriment and Dancing Until 4:30 A.M.

A young lawyer and politician from Ohio named Rutherford B. Hayes wrote these notes about a plantation party that he attended in 1848 at Peach Point Plantation in Texas:

Day spent in talking about and primping up for the party in the evening. At 2 p.m. gentlemen and ladies begin to arrive. Gentlemen and ladies on horseback, through mud and rain, ten, fifteen, or twenty miles. An exceedingly agreeable, gay, and polished company. The ladies particularly noticeable for the possession of the winning qualities. Merriment and dancing until 4:30 a.m. Sleeping arrangements for all got up in all manner of ways, but comfortable.

Slaves on Southern plantations have their own favorite foods. This family is eating hoecakes made with corn flour and a curdled milk dish known as clabber.

chair and visiting is a major social event in the South.

A very interesting aspect of plantation life to witness is the weekly "Drawing," usually held on a Saturday night, when slave families are given their allotment of food for the week by the plantation owner or overseer. A representative from each slave family comes forward and is given a set amount of food that typically includes corn, either on the ear or shucked, some salt, and several pounds of bacon. Rations depend on the wealth, management, and crop yields of the plantation, and on the region. Slaves in the Deep South may also receive pitchers of molasses from the sugar refinery. In Texas, many slaves receive rations of beef and wheat flour. "There plenty meat and tea and coffee and white flour," said one slave about a Texas plantation. "Mammy fix some biscuits. . . . The biscuits was yum, yum, yum to me."[30] The Drawing is a festive time and is anticipated eagerly by slaves.

Another social event that is not to be missed is the Plantation Ball, a lavish party that frequently lasts for days on end and offers a plantation family the chance to show off their mansion—in particular the ballroom, which was built for the occasion—to friends, family, and neighbors. The finest dresses, shoes, and suits are commissioned especially for the occasion, musicians are engaged to play dance music, and tables are laden with special food and drink for the duration of the party.

On a rainy day, when going outdoors is undesirable, your plantation host may open his or her "Noah's Ark" box of hidden treasures. "Perfect deluge of rain," writes Mrs. Isaac H. Hilliard of Grand Lake, Arkansas, in her journal, "so we betake ourselves to my Noah's Ark—alias big cedar chest—crammed with silks, crapes, embroideries, linens, velvets etc.—the extravagance of my girlhood."[31]

Entertainment by Slaves

Plantation owners occasionally entertain guests by summoning their slaves to the Big House at night to perform. Here, and in private gatherings of slaves on weekend nights, slaves continue traditions of music and dance that originated in Africa. You may see dances like the buck-and-wing, or pigeon wing, in which dancers flap their arms and legs while holding their necks and heads stiff, like a bird. Slaves also learn how to dance Irish jigs and cakewalks, in which couples make sharp, precise turns on a designated path. The name comes from the cake that winners receive in a cakewalk competition.

Other dances of slaves that may not be appropriate for the plantation house but are performed in private gatherings include the ring dance, where slaves dance in a circular path and vibrate their entire bodies. The buzzard lope is based on the movements of a turkey buzzard who is trying to capture the attentions of

A slave on a Kentucky plantation plays the banjo as his family enjoys some leisure time. Occasionally, visitors to plantations are treated to an evening of slave music and dance.

a hen, and a water dance is performed with a bucket or glass of water placed on the head. The djouba, or hambone dance, is an exuberant movement punctuated by the slapping of the dancer's legs and chest.

Jefferson noted the similarities of his slaves' banjars, or banjoes, to the European guitar. Slaves play these and fiddles, and beat out rhythms by patting knees, arms, and backs or clinking together spoons or bones.

Chapter 5

Exploring Rural Southern Culture

The inquisitive traveler willing to venture into the countryside will find endless fields and rolling lands interrupted only by thick woods and forests through much of the South. Indeed, you can journey on foot or on horseback for days in some places without encountering a single village or settlement. Olmsted writes:

> For hours and hours one has to ride through the unlimited, continual, all-shadowing, all-embracing forest, following roads in the making of which no more labour has been given than was necessary to remove the timber which would obstruct the passage of wagons; and even for days and days he may sometimes travel, and see never two dwellings of mankind within sight of each other.[32]

It has been said that the genius of the South lies in its rural nature. The unhurried country lifestyle that began in Virginia and has spread throughout the South has become a desired way of life for generations of Southerners. People in the South cherish their connection to the land and the simple pleasures of being outside on a warm day, raising their own food, churchgoing, and entertaining themselves through storytelling and playing music. Many have no interest in keeping abreast of the developments in science, medicine, and machinery of our modern age, nor do they pine for the cultural and intellectual life of cities. As Albert Sidney Johnston, a former soldier who has established the China Grove Plantation in Brazoria County, Texas, writes, "We like our residence here, although entirely secluded from the world and from all society whatever. If we lose the pleasures and sweets of society, we are free from all the drawbacks, which themselves form a numerous catalogue. Happy contentment reigns under our humble roof."[33]

It is no coincidence that some of the South's greatest thinkers and statesmen—George Washington, Thomas Jefferson, James Madison, Zachary Taylor, and Robert E. Lee—chose to raise crops and live in the country rather than settle in a city. As politician John C. Calhoun wrote upon his return to South Carolina in 1849, "The Jessamine and Dogwood were in bloom, and the forest had just commenced clothing itself with green. The contrast was great between being pent up in a boarding house in Washington and breathing the pure fresh air of the country, made fragrant by the blossoms of Spring."[34]

You may find that much of the South is not quite as "civilized" as other places you have visited, in that many people continue to live a simple, agrarian lifestyle with few frills or modern amenities. Be prepared for bewildering directions; lodgings that are not easy to find and may offer only the slimmest of amenities in terms of beds, food, and ser-

Although the urban areas of the South are growing, most Southerners continue to live in rural areas such as this cotton plantation in Mississippi.

Even former president George Washington preferred the quiet of his Mount Vernon plantation to the hustle and bustle of the city.

vices for your horses; and foods that can range from the most basic fare to sumptuous feasts. You will be rewarded by the very essence of Southern culture, and a glimpse at an unhurried lifestyle that is quickly disappearing from other parts of the country.

Meet Your Hosts: Yeomen and Crackers

Outside of the large plantations, where the South's richest families dwell, the people you will meet in rural areas are likely to occupy the Southern middle and lower classes. As you travel through the South you will meet far more people who occupy these positions in Southern society than you will rich planters.

The South's middle class are called yeomen. Typically they are landowners who have modest plots of land that yield enough food to keep the yeoman and his family comfortably fed throughout the year. A small garden near the home supplies the family with vegetables and greens, and a larger plot is planted with the rows of corn that constitute a staple of the yeoman's diet. Not being bound to spending the majority of his time growing food or making money, the yeoman enjoys a variety of other pursuits, including fishing and hunting, the latter with one of the dogs invariably found lounging in the yards and homes of their masters.

Yeomen may own one or two slaves, but for the most part, yeomen are not slave owners. Their homes are simple and comfortable, consisting typically of log cabins that are occasionally chinked but more often not. The cabins are frequently built in a distinctive style peculiar to the South that consists of two rooms connected by an open, covered breezeway that acts as a porch. The windows to these cabins are open to the elements, sometimes with oil paper to keep out the drafts and vermin, but no

glass. Inside these rough cabins, you will find a few pieces of old-fashioned heirloom furniture and frequently a single, expensive piece of furniture such as a standing clock that is cherished by the family.

Barely educated, proud as can be of their Southern heritage, and happy to do as little serious work as needed, the yeomen are a curious lot. "They [live] in almost unbelievable disorder," writes one observer. "Nearly all of them [enjoy] some measure of a kind of curious half-thrifty, half-shiftless prosperity—a thing of sagging rail fences, unpainted houses, and crazy barns which yet bulge with corn."[35]

You Can't Get There from Here

Southerners' explanations of how to find your way can be confusing. Consider these directions that Frederick Law Olmsted received on how to find a plantation house in Virginia on horseback, as recorded in his book, *The Cotton Kingdom: A Traveller's Observations on Cotton and Slavery*:

You take this road here—you'll see where it's most traveled, and it's easy enough to keep on it for about a mile; then there's a fork, and you take the right; pretty soon, you'll cross a creek and turn to the right—the creek's been up a good deal lately, and there's some big trees fallen along there, and if they ha'n't got them out of the way, you may have some difficulty in finding where the road is; but you keep bearing off to the right, where it's the most open, and you'll see it again pretty soon. Then you go on, keeping along in the road—you'll see where folks have traveled before—for may be a quarter of a mile, and you'll find a cross road; you must take that to the left; pretty soon you'll pass two cabins; one of 'em's old and all fallen in, the other one's new, and there's a white man lives into it: you can't mistake it. About a hundred yards beyond it, there's a fork, and you take the left—it turns square off, and it's fenced for a good bit; keep along by the fence, and you can't miss it.

Slaves pick cotton on a Mississippi plantation while others transport huge bales of the crop. Although wealthy planters typically own dozens of slaves, most small farmers own just one or two.

Other writers, however, admire the yeoman's "manly independence of character" and ability to earn an honest livelihood from his own toil.

The South's rural poor are variously known as hillbillies, squatters, or crackers. These names may seem derogatory, but they are widely accepted throughout the South, and even used by the crackers themselves. The "cracker" title simply derives from their habit of frequently cracking their whips when they come into town from their homes deep in the woods or hills of the rural South. They have a distinctive appearance: "Single-breasted coats without collars, broad-brimmed and low-crowned hats, and gray hair floating in loose locks over their shoulders, were among their peculiarities,"[36] writes one Southerner.

Other observers have not been as kind. Much has been written about their poverty, filth, lack of ambition, and physical abnormalities. Many believe implicitly in witchcraft and attribute everything that happens, good or bad, to the agency of persons whom they suppose are possessed of evil spirits.

Seasonal Activities in the Rural South

The South enjoys four seasons of the year, but rural Southern seasons are based more on the agricultural cycle than on the traditional seasons of spring, summer, fall, and winter. The months of March, April, and May are devoted to planting and preparing the soil for the next year's crop. The hot summer is the growing season, where the corn, cotton, and sugarcane plants grow tall under the blazing sun. Fall brings all available hands to the fields for harvest, the busiest time of year. Besides reaping the crops from the field, the produce must be processed, at gins and mills in the case of cotton and sugar, packaged and baled, and sent off to markets around the world.

Autumn also is the time to prepare the household for the winter months. At this time of year, parts of the South celebrate festivals of hog killing in order to store up enough meat for the rest of the year.

In December, everyone relaxes during the end-of-year holiday season, when the Christmas and New Year's holidays are celebrated. Slaves and field hands are given a week off, and gifts of clothing, food, cash, and toys are distributed by plantation owners to all hands.

Things to Do

The rural South has unique entertainments, festivals, and sights to see. You will spend long hours riding or traveling over rudimentary country roads, enjoying the scenery of woods and modest farms, and you will soak up country culture at the homes and lodgings that you secure at the end of each day. The rural South may not have the cultural entertainments such as opera and theater that you will find in the cities, but there are many unique things to see, and traditional Southern gatherings that you should attempt to experience. Try to include some of the following during your travels to experience Southern culture firsthand:

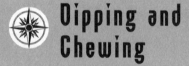

Dipping and Chewing

Tobacco use is quite popular in the South, particularly in Virginia and North Carolina, where tobacco is widely grown, and you will be offered tobacco in many forms. One of the favorite pastimes of rural Southerners at the end of the day is to sit on the porch, tell stories and "dip" into the tobacco bag to chew tobacco or inhale "snuff," which is powderized tobacco. Snuff is especially popular among poor, rural women of the South. "Pray put your snuff box aside when you are working over your butter," implored the Farmer's Almanack of 1815. The sharing of snuff is an inexpensive way for poorer people to extend hospitality to travelers. "Among the country people [of North Carolina], the proffer of the snuff-box, and its passing from hand to hand is the usual civility," wrote one English traveler.

Visit the University of Virginia in Charlottesville. Jefferson revolutionized the concept of a college campus when he designed this, the South's greatest university, late in his life. The campus is centered around a library, not a chapel, and its ten Romanesque pavilions house distinguished faculty upstairs, with classrooms downstairs. The library itself resembles Rome's Pantheon, with its tall dome suggesting the grandeur of human achievement. When it opened thirty years ago, the university enrolled 123 students (one famous student was Edgar Allen Poe, who attended in 1826–1827); enrollment has grown dramatically since then. Known widely as the "pride of Virginia," the university recently added engineering to its fields of study, previously consisting of liberal arts, medicine, and law. The incidence of rowdy behavior among students has dropped significantly since 1840, when a law professor was shot and killed by a student, at which time students adopted an honor system and agreed to "vouch" for each other's conduct and report misbehavior.

Attend a Husking Bee. When the corn crop is in, the all-important job of husking begins to remove the corncobs from their protective green coverings in order to allow the corn to dry and not mold. Friends, neighbors, and even

Slaves on Southern plantations often combine work and pleasure. Those pictured here are singing as they shuck corn at a husking bee.

passing travelers are called together to get the husking job done quickly, and most husking bees become raucous parties. As one Kentucky man reported, "When the crop was drawn in, the ears were heaped into a long pile or rick, a night fixed on, and the neighbors notified, rather than invited, for it was an affair of mutual assistance. As they assembled at nightfall, the green glass quart whiskey bottle, stopped with a cob, was handed to every one, man and boy, as they arrived, to take a drink."[37]

Experience a Virginia Mineral Spring. Want to meet a cross section of influential Southerners, from judges and politicians to prominent businessmen and planters? Head to White Sulphur Springs in the Appalachian mountains of western Virginia, near the town of Roanoke, during the hot summer months. Here, the upper crust of Southern society has been meeting since the late-eighteenth century to bathe in and drink the sulfurous mineral waters that are said to have healing properties. Many business deals have been completed here, not to mention engagements between the young couples who promenade at night through the resort. "Here you have a fine chance to see Southern beauty and mingle in Southern society," wrote one visitor to a friend. "The greatest harmony and intercourse prevail throughout. Balls every night."[38] And good news for visitors who stay in the rows of cabins known as Paradise Row, Baltimore Row, and Al-

abama Row: A grand new hotel has just opened, offering ultraluxurious accommodations to guests who make the difficult journey through the forests via horseback or stagecoach.

Go to a Mississippi Plank Dance. The high point of many a social gathering in Mississippi is the Plank Dance, where partners face each other and do a fast jig atop a plank that has been laid between two barrels. As lively music is played from a fiddle and a banjo, the dancers step lively as the other partygoers crowd around them and shout encouraging words like, "Keep it up, John! Go it Nance! Heel and toe, and ketch a fire!"

Visit Southern Potters. The art of pottery flourishes throughout the South. Look for "jugtowns" in Georgia, Alabama, and North Carolina where pottery is created by skilled craftsmen. In North Carolina, the Cole and Craven families have been throwing pots for nearly a century: Some claim that their distinctive glazes include tobacco juice. In Edgefield, South Carolina, look for the work of Dave, a Slave, an actual slave who inscribes his pots with poetry, such as "Dave belongs to Mr. Miles/wher the oven bakes & the pot biles," or "Great & noble Jar/hold Sheep goat or bear."

Experience a Southern Christmas and "Storming." Christmas morning in the rural South begins with slaves and family members rousing each other from bed

On Christmas morning, it is customary for slaves to toast the health of their masters. The festivities then continue as family and friends come together for a lavish party.

with shouts of "Christmas gift! Christmas gift!" Foaming cups of eggnog are produced and drunk, and gifts are exchanged. Parties are held with music and dancing, and neighbors and family members get together to enjoy a day of "storming," or visiting nearby homes where parties are being held.

You may be surprised to see that the German tradition of placing and decorating a tree inside the home for Christmas has recently begun in some Southern households. Mrs. Mahala Eggleston Roach of Vicksburg, Mississippi, began the practice a few years ago when she surprised her family and neighbors with a Christmas tree. "Mother, Aunt and Liz came down to see it," she writes. "All said it was something new to them. I never saw one but learned [of it] from some of the German stories I had been reading."[39]

Food and Lodging for the Rural Traveler

Finding adequate food and shelter can be a daily trial for a traveler through the rural areas of the South. Many planters refuse to take in travelers, and you may find yourself riding well into the evening hours before you find a hospitable lodging. Begin your search well before the sun sets by asking field hands and people along the road about inns or travelers' rests in the area.

Standards for food and sleeping accommodations vary widely, and the traveler must take what he is offered. In some places the fare will consist solely of cornmeal and pork, or variations of each, such as the hominy grits, a corn-based grain, that are widely served in the South. "Hog and hominy, and corn-cake, for breakfast; waffles, hog and hominy for dinner; and hog, hominy,

and corn-cake for supper,"[40] wrote one recent visitor to the Inn at Georgetown, South Carolina. In Georgia, another traveler was treated to a veritable jackpot of a dinner that included hot biscuit and corn cakes, fried fowl, fried bacon and eggs and cold ham, preserved peaches, preserved quinces and grapes, followed by hot wheaten biscuit, and hot shortcake and hot corn cake and hot griddle cakes, soaked in butter; coffee, milk sour or sweet; and molasses poured freely on cakes and bacon.

Sleeping accommodations might consist of a pile of shredded corn husks on a dirt floor, or a warm bed in a private room with a hot fire. Outside of Raleigh, Virginia, for example, a traveler should seek out the house of a Mrs. Barclay, where supper can include seven kinds of pork, two of maize, wheat cakes, broiled quails, cold roast turkey, coffee and tea, and you sleep in a private bedroom with a broad fireplace, a stuffed easy chair, and a tub of hot water to soak your weary feet. For this, Mrs. Barclay charges a dollar a night.

In certain parts of western Louisiana, you may have to make do with a plate of cold, salt fat pork; a cup of what seems to be lard but the proprietor calls butter; a plate of very stale, dry, flaky cornbread; a jug of molasses, and a pitcher of milk. The beverages may not be much better. As Olmsted writes of one morning beverage, "A black decoction known as coffee makes it difficult to imagine any beverage more revolting."[41] Lovers of meat will enjoy traveling in Texas, where the fare almost exclusively consists of barbecued meats. "These Texans are essentially carnivorous," writes visiting lawyer Rutherford B. Hayes of Ohio in his journal. "Pork ribs, pigs' feet, veal, beef (grand), chickens, venison, and dried meat frequently seen on the table at once."[42]

If by chance you are invited to dine with slaves in their quarters, you will experience another distinctive type of Southern fare. Slave food tends to be simple and repetitive. Cornmeal is mixed with water to make cornpone. Ash pone is a coarse corn cake baked in the ashes of a fire, which typically serves as a substitute for flour bread. Hoe cake is another cornmeal cake that consists of cornpone that is spread onto a hoe and baked over the coals. Chitlins or chitterlings are the small intestines of hogs, usually cut into small pieces and fried to a crispy finish. Cracklin' bread is corn bread mixed with fried hog fat that contains "cracklins," or bits of fried pork. Collards are greens that are cooked in water. If they are cooked long enough, the water takes on a distinctive color and flavor and is known pot likker.

Rural Southern Speech and Expressions

Southern speech is distinct, with its own rhythms, expressions, and vocabulary. Many rural Southerners speak with a pronounced drawl that may be difficult to understand at first hearing.

People use different expressions when dealing with travelers in different parts of the South. In the cotton districts, for example, the salutation if you cross paths with a man is, *How d'ye do, sir* (never Good Morning). On parting it is, *I wish you well, sir* (not Good-bye). In the western part of the South, you may in many places be spoken to roughly, such as when you are called to supper by a direct statement such as, *come in to supper* or *take a seat*. In many homes, your hosts will call you *Stranger* or *Friend*, even if they know your name. The exception to this is Texas, where people pride themselves on remembering names. And if some, one asks if your horse or dog is *ill*, they do not wish to know if it is sick. *Ill* is used for vicious, and "Is your horse ill?" really means to ask if it will bite a stranger.

Travel Tip: Careening Hogs Spell Danger

Keep an eye out for wild pigs. Hogs run wild and free throughout much of the South, and there are millions of them. They may emerge from underbrush or woods in groups of three to a dozen, and they are nearly always moving at a full gallop, looking straight ahead, and emitting a series of rapid grunts. They can literally bowl over a rider and a horse, and can be quite dangerous if cornered.

Finding suitable accommodations in the rural areas of the South can be a challenge. Some travelers have complained their lodgings were no nicer than these slave quarters.

If you are asked to *acknowledge the corn*, you must confess and admit the truth. Need a stiff drink after a hard day of riding? Ask for an *anti-fogmatic*, which is raw rum or whiskey. If you change your mind a lot, you may be accused of *backing and filling*. If someone says "this hot weather makes a *body* feel bad," they don't mean a corpse. A *body* is a person. If you overindulge with the bourbon or whiskey, you may be said to have a *brick in your hat* (you are drunk), or more simply, you are *corned*. If you walk a *Virginia fence*, it probably means you are drunk and staggering and following a zigzag line.

The time of day when the light grows dim is known, appropriately, as *candlelighting*. If someone is beaten badly in a fight, they are *catawamptiously chawed up*, and folks who make too much money and have *highfalutin'* (snobbish and condescending) ways about them belong to the *codfish aristocracy*. A *coon's age* is a very long time, and if someone wants to get even with you, they'll *fix your flint*. Watch out for the

Appalachian Speech

Southerners who live in the hill country of western Virginia, Tennessee, and Georgia have their own distinctive pronunciations and figures of speech. Use this list to help translate their words:

WHAT THEY SAY	WHAT THEY MEAN
Acrost	Across
Afeared	Afraid
Agin	Against
Aim	Intend, mean
Backards	Backwards
Brung	Brought
Call	Reason
Didje	Did you
Druther	I'd rather
Fitten	Appropriate
Fixen	Intending
Heerd	Heard
Hisn, Hern	His, Hers
Holler	Valley
Lasses	Molasses
Law, Laws	The Lord
Ourn	Ours
Poke	Bag
Richeer	Right here
Spell	For a time
Tother	The other
Uppity	Snobbish
Vittles	Food
Widder	Widow
Yaller	Yellow
Yourn	Yours

gallnippers (huge mosquitoes) in the summertime. They can make you look peaked (thin or sickly in appearance).

In Baltimore, keep a wary eye out for the plug-uglys, or local hooligans; in Missouri, they are known as the pukes. Hey, loudmouth, shut pan and sing small, or shut your mouth. Get too noisy and you can wake snakes. If you really like what someone did or you admire their horse, you might say they are some pumpkins. Nobody in polite company wants to hear about your pants or trousers, but they will know what you mean when you refer to your inexpressibles, nether garments or sit-down-upons.

Chapter 6

Exploring the South's Major Cities

The South's major cities are bustling centers of commerce, where the products of Southern agriculture are brokered and shipped, and where millions of dollars change hands. Manufacturing concerns are also growing in the cities, employing thousands of workers and producing goods that are shipped all over the world.

Besides the commercial side of city life, the South's cities are centers of social life and the arts. Theater, music, and opera are important cultural components of city life, and high society has a full schedule of parties, balls, and social events. Each city has a unique design and architectural style, and the residents are urbane, cultured, and immaculately dressed in the latest fashions. Wealthy planters who live and work in the country make a point of visiting the cities every year, with families and servants in tow, for rounds of parties and balls, and to announce and attend the engagements and weddings of high society. Charleston, Richmond, and New Orleans, the newcomer on the commercial scene of the South, are the South's showplaces.

Exploring Charleston

The choicest society of the South is in Charleston, the handsome city that occupies a narrow peninsula between the Ashley and Cooper rivers on the South Carolina coast. The city of forty-one thousand has become an important hub of manufacturing and commerce; it is also regarded as the South's preeminent center of theater and social life. Despite fires that have ravaged the city three times, hurricanes that sweep through and wreak havoc, and the annual threat of pestilence (just last year, yellow

Visitors to Charleston, South Carolina, can stroll along broad streets such as the one pictured here, visiting graceful churches and elegant homes.

fever-carrying mosquitoes created an outbreak that killed 627 people), Charleston is the jewel of Southern cities. As an eighteenth-century visitor wrote, "An European at his first arrival must be greatly surprised when he sees the elegance of their houses, their sumptuous furniture, as well as the magnificence of their tables."[43]

As a hub of commerce and export in the 1820s, Charleston exported over 200,000 bales of cotton a year and shipped enormous crops of rice from South Carolina plantations. A devastat-

ing fire leveled the city in 1835, but Charleston began to rebuild immediately. Charleston is the manufacturing center of South Carolina, with fourteen grist mills, six rice mills, six iron foundries, including the Phoenix Iron Works, six turpentine distilleries, a railroad machine shop and depot, and numerous sawmills. The city also houses umbrella factories, a cordage factory, a hatmaker, and manufacturers of organs, stained glass, silverware, railway cars, carriages and wagons, brickyards, and tinware shops. This year, as many as

Cities along the Southern coast serve as hubs of commerce. Here, a group of slaves is waving to friends riding on a barge loaded with cotton bales.

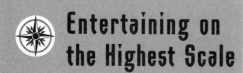

Entertaining on the Highest Scale

Be ready to be treated to the most extravagant food and drink, in enormous quantities, if you are invited to a society party in Charleston. A Mrs. Charles Aston set the standard a few years ago, when in February 1851 she threw a splendid ball that did not end until the 200 guests had used 18 dozen plates, 14 dozen knives, 28 dozen spoons, and 6 dozen champagne glasses, all used to consume 4 turkeys, 4 hams, 50 partridges, 12 pheasants, 22 ducks, 10 quarts of oysters, 4 pyramids of crystallized fruit and coconut, and "immense quantities" of bonbons, cakes, creams, and jellies.

449,500 bales of cotton are expected to enter the city by rail and leave by ship.

Charleston has long been an active supporter of theater. In 1773, when a new theater opened, the city witnessed 118 performances in the first year alone, including Shakespearean tragedies and popular operas. That theater burned down, but in 1837, citizens raised sixty thousand dollars to build the New Charleston Theatre on the west side of Meeting Street between Market Street and Horlbeck Alley. The imposing Greek revival edifice accommodates twelve hundred patrons for shows that are managed by William Abbott, an English impresario. The Charleston Library Society was founded over a century ago, in 1748, and circulates

books. The Apprentices' Library Society has two thousand books, mostly on religion, with biographies and novels with themes of moral uplift. The Charleston Port Society lends books for "floating libraries" for mariners on vessels. The *Charleston Mercury* is one of the leading newspapers of the South.

The city is a leading center of education for young people. The private High School of Charleston, established in 1839, charges an annual tuition of forty dollars and educates the sons of the South's rich. The Orphan House provides public education. There are a number of private academies for girls, as well as dancing masters and music teachers. Madam Ann Marsan Talvande's French School for the Young Ladies is an exclusive establishment that teaches arts and sciences, dancing, piano, guitar, and singing. It is the finest and most expensive finishing school in the city. Located near the corner of Legare and Tradd streets, the school is surrounded by a high brick wall topped with broken glass to keep out unwelcome intruders.

Things to Do in Charleston

Social life is so prominent in Charleston that many planters from the surrounding region and as far north as Virginia would not dream of missing a winter society season of balls, dinner parties, and events. The St. Cecilia Society, founded in 1762 for musical concerts, keeps things busy by scheduling the most exclusive private parties in the South. As a visitor, try to get invited to a big party, and take advantage of some of these unique features of Charleston:

Drink Syllabub at Christmas. A delicious drink peculiar to Charleston that consists of white wine, brandy, sugar, and whipped cream, syllabub is something like eggnog. Be careful of its rather sneaky powers of intoxication.

Promenade on the Lower Peninsula. Charleston's elite live at White Point, where a stroller will be treated to gardens with beautiful pagodas and broad and serpentine walks along the Battery. The Ashley River is on one side, and large and picturesque old homes are on the other. Take a look at the new mansion built in 1850 by planter Thomas Aston Coffin on One East Battery, the best site in the city. Its three stories have tiers of piazzas that offer a magnificent view of both the Ashley and Cooper rivers and the harbor. The air is perfumed with the blossoms of orange and jasmine trees.

Notice the Distinctive Single Houses. "In Charleston, persons vie with one another, not who shall have the finest, but who the coolest house,"[44] wrote one visitor. The answer is the Single House, a narrow, rectangular building, just one

Teacher

room deep, whose short side faces the street and whose broad side features wide, covered porches at each level that are oriented to catch prevailing breezes during the hot summer months.

Stay in a Fine Hotel. The Mills House is a five-story structure at the corner of Meeting and Queen Streets. It is famed for its wine cellar and cuisine, costly in furniture, rich in decorations, and favored by the all-fashionable gentry. Less ornate but comfortable are Planter's Hotel on Queen Street and the Charleston Hotel on Meeting Street.

Travel Tip: The Luxury of Running Water and Steam Heat

Would you like to experience both running water and steam heat (a rarity in these times) under one roof? Visit Charleston's beautiful new Mills House on Meeting Street, recently opened in 1853 and named for Otis Mills, known locally as "the Jacob Astor of Charleston." Its lavish modern conveniences make it the preeminent meetinghouse in the South.

People seeking accommodations in Charleston should stay at The Mills House. The five-story hotel on Meeting Street offers guests luxurious rooms and modern conveniences.

Avoid "the Neck." During the summer months in particular, avoid Charleston's gritty, industrial north side that is known as the Neck. Besides being a rougher part of town, it is also considered to be the breeding grounds for the diseases that periodically decimate the city's population. A local saying is, "To sleep on the Neck between the first of June and frost [is] . . . tantamount to ordering one's coffin."[45]

Exploring New Orleans

Founded in 1718, Louisiana's port city began with a bad reputation. It was originally settled in part by inmates from French jails. The city was passed back and forth between political powers in its early years. Ceded to England and Spain in 1763, when the population was only a few thousand, it reverted to French ownership in 1803. Sold shortly afterward to the United States in the Louisiana Purchase, it witnessed a major battle with the British in 1815 to conclude the War of 1812. Since then, New Orleans has enjoyed unprecedented growth, and with 116,000 people counted in the census of 1850, it has become the largest city in the South.

New Orleans' vigorous growth stems from its location at the mouth of the Mississippi River, America's greatest trade route. Here, the goods of the North meet the enormous (and enormously profitable) bounty of the cotton states, and fortunes are made in the brokerage and shipping of goods, as well as the banking of the profits they supply. New Orleans is one of the most ethnically diverse capitals in the world. The long-established French and Spanish families have been joined by Yankees, Jews, Germans, and Irishmen who came down the Mississippi to get a piece of the trade in New Orleans, joining the Acadians, or Cajuns, who settled the surrounding bayou.

In New Orleans you will actually find two cities in one. The first is the Vieux Carré, or French Quarter, the oldest part of the city, which vividly displays its French influence. It is a place of distinctive two- and three-story homes with elaborate wrought-iron railings, and gardens that spill forth with oleander, wisteria, camellia, banana, and yucca plants.

The city of New Orleans boasts one of the busiest ports in the world. Every day, ships laden with cotton leave its docks, bound for destinations throughout the world.

Public buildings include the cathedral, the Hotel Royal with a slave market that is one of the busiest in the South, and the Opera House, which is home to the mask balls that the locals adore, particularly during the festival season known as Mardi Gras.

The other half of New Orleans is the "American" city, a place of warehouses, cotton compresses, wharves, shops, and banks that constitute the robust commercial heart of the city. Here you will find the Garden District, a genteel place of plantation homes that borrow on the style of other plantation mansions, with tall columns announcing entryways, broad verandahs, and exquisite gardens.

The people of New Orleans lead a lively social life and enjoy one of the most distinctive and satisfying cuisines in the country. Their parties and balls are renowned, and their hospitality is legendary.

Street Life

You may be surprised to see that New Orleans is far less dependent on slave labor than much of the rest of the South. Many laborers whom you encounter in public are free men, and unlike most places in the South, many jobs are done by white immigrants. The majority of the cartmen, hackney coachmen, porters, railroad hands, public waiters, and common laborers, as well as the skilled mechanics, are white; of the Negroes employed in those professions, a considerable number are free.

White and black people walk the streets together, and it is not uncommon to see white and black alike dressed in the finest clothes from Paris. A surprised Olmsted wrote:

In what I suppose to be the fashionable streets, there were many more well-dressed and highly-dressed coloured people than white; and among this dark gentry the finest French cloths, embroidered waistcoats, patent-leather shoes, resplendent brooches, silk hats, kid gloves, and eau de mille fleurs, were quite common. . . . Many of the coloured ladies were dressed not only expensively, but with good taste and effect, after the latest Parisian mode. Some of them were very attractive in appearance, and would have produced a decided sensation in any European drawing-room.[46]

Things to Do in New Orleans

New Orleans is a great place to walk, with interesting architecture on every street, the bustle of commerce and shops, and wonderful food. Try to experience some of these attractions during your visit:

Eat Gumbo and Oysters. New Orleans' distinctive cuisine is a delicious combination of French, Creole, and Cajun influences. Many roadhouses, taverns, and restaurants can supply you with a rich, satisfying bowl of gumbo, a hearty soup, or stew distinctive to the city. "It is a kind of save-all, salmagundi soup, made of the ends of every variety of flesh, mingled with rice, and seasoned with chopped sassafras, or with okra, a vegetable esculent,"[47] wrote one visitor.

For a special treat, try the local oysters. The shellfish that have become a delicacy in dinner parties throughout the South are available in profusion in New Orleans, and are prepared in a number of tasty ways. Here, they are sold on the streets from carts, in oyster rooms, in

Racial Categorization in New Orleans

Intermingling of the races is so common in New Orleans that the French created a formula and a vocabulary to categorize the locals' racial status. One's title, and social class, is determined by calculating one's white and nonwhite ancestry over eight generations, a total of 128 people.

White Ancestors	Nonwhite Ancestors	Racial Title
128	0	White
127	1	Sang Melee
120	8	Mamelouque
112	16	Metif or Octoroon
96	32	Quadroon
64	64	Mulatto
48	80	Marabou
32	96	Griffe
16	112	Sacatra
0	128	Negro

The Plantation South

saloons, and in restaurants. They are broiled, boiled, deviled, curried, fricasseed, fried, scalloped, steamed, stewed, and put into omelettes and Po' Boy sandwiches (an oyster sandwich with a tangy sauce on a freshly baked roll). Locals like to eat their oysters at the Gem Restaurant with a hot sauce that was created by local merchant Maunsel White.

Visit the Place d'Armes. The finest public garden in the city is a delightful, peaceful place of orange and lemon trees, rose bushes, myrtles and laurels, and jasmines from the south of France. Fronting the garden is the Hotel de Ville, the city's quaint, French-influenced courthouse that has been described as being among the most picturesque public buildings in

This photograph shows an extremely busy scene along New Orleans's Canal Street. New Orleans is the largest city in the South, with well over 100,000 residents.

Public Notice to a Mask Ball

To attend a mask ball in New Orleans, look for advertisements in the newspaper like this one that recently announced a party that was open to the public.

THE GLOBE BALL ROOM
Corner of St. Claude and St. Peter Streets, abreast of the Old Basin,

WILL OPEN THIS EVENING, October 16, when a Society Ball will be given.

No ladies admitted without masks.

Gentlemen, fifty cents—Ladies, gratis. Doors open at 9 ½ o'clock. Ball to commence at 10 o'clock.

No person admitted with weapons, by order of the Council.

A superior orchestra has been engaged for the season.

The public may be assured of the most strict order, as there will be at all times an efficient police in attendance.

Attached to the establishment is a superior Bar, well stocked with wines and liquors; also, a Restaurant, where may be had all such delicacies as the market affords.

All ladies are requested to procure free tickets in the Mask Room, as no lady will be admitted into the ball-room without one.

A. WHITLOCK,
Manager

the country. Adjoining the courthouse is an ancient Spanish cathedral with a simple, unadorned design that may appear odd in the local scheme of highly decorated and embellished houses and public buildings.

Attend a Mardi Gras Celebration. If you visit New Orleans in the winter or spring, be sure to attend the festivities of Mardi Gras, the annual celebration leading up to Lent. Beginning in December, New Orleans society hosts a number of balls to honor the season's debutantes, as well as any number of supper, breakfast, and dinner dances, and cocktail parties. During the week leading up to Fat Tuesday (Mardi Gras in French), the whole city bursts out with celebrations. A parade that was first held in 1837 features colorful floats and puppets designed and built by local parishes. Recently, a fraternal organization called the Mystik Krewe of Comus began to hold impromptu torchlight parades at night during Mardi Gras week. Participants dress in the most outlandish and provocative costumes and engage in spirited dancing and clowning. These parades are wildly successful, and are centered on Canal Street. The revelry and music are loud and raucous, growing to a fever pitch on Fat Tuesday. When midnight comes, signaling the beginning of Ash Wednesday, the parades end, the crowds scatter, and the streets return to normal.

Have a Drink at the Hotel St. Louis. One of the city's finest hotels is also one of its top spots to have a refreshing drink and mingle with some of Louisiana's wealthiest planters. Built around a lofty rotunda with a towering dome, the bar is paved with marble, with an enormous, semicircular bar, also of marble. Here, planters gather to drink, conduct business, and socialize before catching a steamboat upriver to their estates.

Exploring Richmond

"Richmond, at a glance from adjacent high ground, through a dull cloud of bituminous smoke, upon a lowering winter's day, has a very picturesque appearance,"[48] wrote Olmsted of his first view of Virginia's capital city, which lies at the head

People go about their business along High Street in Richmond, Virginia. The city is one of the most industrialized in the South, with an iron foundry and two major railroad lines.

of the James River, 100 miles (161km) south of Washington, D.C. Many travelers through the South will wind up here at one point, because Richmond is the terminus of two major Southern railroad systems. The city of twenty-eight thousand is a cosmopolitan center of tobacco warehouses and heavy industry, including Tredegar Iron Works, the South's major foundry. Its mixed population includes a considerable number of immigrants from Europe and freed slaves. Coal that is mined in western Virginia is shipped from here to all of the major cities of the Atlantic seaboard.

Richmond is a busy, bustling place, where streets are ruled by large wagons drawn by six mules, with a teamster who rides on the back of the near-wheeler. The city's canals are crowded with long, narrow, canoelike boats, perhaps 50 feet (15m) long and 6 (3m) wide, that draw very little water and are loaded with tobacco, flour, and a great variety of raw country produce. Navigation is by poling the boat through the canal. The canal district is gritty and coarse, with many eating and drinking shops of the lowest level that cater to Negroes and boatmen, but much of Richmond is elegant and prosperous, reflecting the tastes of the plantation owners and businessmen who come here for the winter social season.

Things to Do in Richmond

Richmond is the political and economic center of Virginia, and many of its attractions lie in those arenas.

Visit the Capitol. The State Capitol, the model of which was obtained by Jefferson from France, is an imposing, Grecian edifice that is topped by a magnificent dome. A grand entrance on the west side is reached by heavy stone steps, leading to a central rotunda whose doors and hallways lead to the legislative offices and chambers of the state's politicians. It is one of the great public buildings of America, and well worth a visit.

Read Richmond's newspapers. The *Enquirer* and the *Whig* are the leading proponents of a brand of Southern journalism that is fiery, provocative, and political. Each takes its stand on the issues of the day in the most searing prose, and defends its issues to the extent of the editors of each paper engaging in numerous duels of honor. Jennings Wise of the *Enquirer* is said to have fought (and won) eight duels in his first two years as editor. That passion is conveyed in the editorials of the papers. For literary writing, the *Southern Literary Messenger* is a magazine that is based in Richmond and carries the finest writing of the day to homes across the South. It was once edited by the novelist Poe.

Stay at The American. We recommend The American, a fine hotel run by New Yorker Milberger Smith, as among the best in the South. The staff is expertly trained to attend to your every need and have that special quality, sometimes difficult to find, of knowing when to enter

The Plantation South

your room and lay out your toilet, linen, and dressing gear, and when to leave you alone. Fires are promptly lit upon request, and boots are polished and ready to go in the morning. The valet staff is composed of Negroes and the dining room servers of Irishmen, and both do their jobs admirably well.

Visit the Slave Market. The most prominent slave market in the country is in Richmond. Here, Negroes are auctioned off to the highest bidder. Many will be "sold south," to the cotton plantations of Mississippi and Louisiana. The Auction House is located in a squalid part of town on Franklin Street, near the post office and a large livery and stable. Side streets in the area house a number of establishments for slave dealers, with prominent signs announcing their businesses. In an auction at the market, slaves young and old, including women and children, are examined closely by traders and prospective buyers. They are poked and prodded, ordered to open their mouths to reveal

No visitor to Richmond should miss the splendid state capitol building. Richmond became the state capital in 1780, and construction on the building began in 1785.

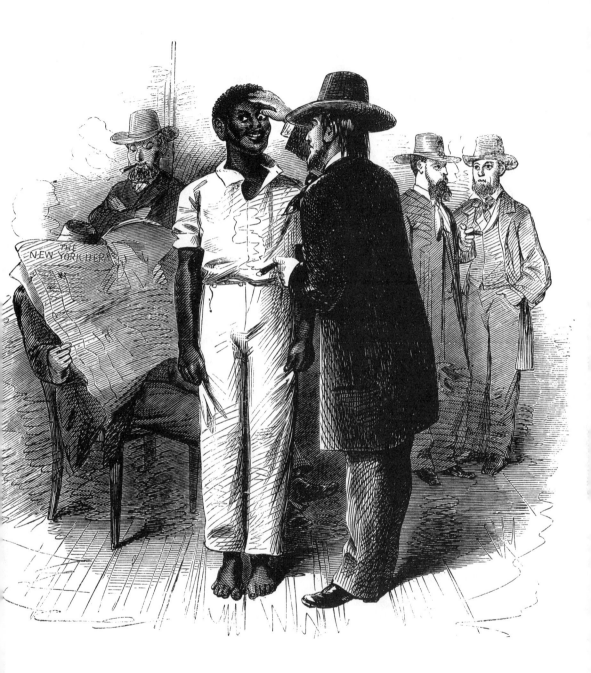

A plantation owner inspects the physical health of a slave at an auction. Visitors interested in slave auctions should be sure to visit the slave market in Richmond.

their teeth and pull up pant legs to show their leg muscles. The highest bidder leads them away.

Cities to Enjoy and Cities to Avoid

Savannah, Georgia, is another city well worth visiting. A bustling seaport of twenty thousand residents, it boasts lovely public parks and a distinctive architecture, and is the center of Georgia's busy lumber industry. Over a half-million bales of cotton are shipped from Savannah to the world's markets each year. Although barely twenty years old, Atlanta, Georgia, is becoming a hub of manufacturing due to its location as the southern terminus of the Western and Atlantic Railroad.

We cannot recommend traveling to some cities in the South. Columbus, North Carolina, for example, a mill town on the Chattahoochee River, has received many critical reviews from disappointed visitors. One traveler reported that he had never seen so much gambling, intoxication, and cruel treatment of servants in public as in Columbus. On a recent visit, Olmsted griped that "The hotel in which I lodged was disgustingly dirty; the table revolting; the waiters stupid, inattentive, and annoying."[49] It was widely reputed to be the best hotel in town.

Norfolk, Virginia, is renowned for its fine harbor, but its public health is dubious, and it has been called a swampy, uncomfortable, disagreeable place. Mobile, Alabama, has a public square that is used as a horse and hog pasture. The city is very expensive, and you will not find a single hatter anywhere. In Memphis, Tennessee, the Commercial Hotel plays a cruel trick on travelers. Its restaurant menu features dozens of delicious items such as beef heart egg sauce, barbecued rabbits, bear sausages, and cheese macaroni, but they are invariably out of everything but greasy cabbage and bacon served in a large, dreary room that looks like a hospital ward. Please adjust your expectations accordingly, or look elsewhere for comforts.

Notes

Introduction: A Culture All Its Own
1. Quoted in Henry Wiencek, *Plantations of the Old South*. Birmingham, AL: Oxmoor House, 1988, p. 13.
2. Quoted in Katharine M. Jones, *The Plantation South*. Indianapolis: The Bobbs-Merrill Company, 1957, p. 236.
3. Quoted in Jones, *The Plantation South*, p. 277.
4. Quoted in Frederick Law Olmsted, *The Cotton Kingdom: A Traveller's Observations on Cotton and Slavery*. New York: Alfred A. Knopf, 1953, p. 259.

Chapter 1: A Brief History of the South
5. Quoted in Francis Butler Simkins, *A History of the South*. New York: Alfred A. Knopf, 1963, p. 20.
6. Quoted in Simkins, *A History of the South*, p. 21.
7. Quoted in Henry Savage Jr., *Discovering America 1700–1875*. New York: Harper & Row, 1979, p. 15.
8. Quoted in Savage, *Discovering America 1700–1875*, p. 23.
9. Quoted in Simkins, *A History of the South*, p. 80.

Chapter 2: The Geography and Climate of the South
10. Quoted in Olmsted, *The Cotton Kingdom*, p. 113.

11. Quoted in Jones, *The Plantation South*, p. 356.
12. Olmsted, *The Cotton Kingdom*, p. 177.
13. Quoted in Isabella G. Leland, *Charleston, Crossroads of History*. Woodland Hills, CA: Windsor, 1980, p. 31.
14. Quoted in Jones, *The Plantation South*, p. 366.
15. Quoted in Jones, *The Plantation South*, p. 363.

Chapter 3: Getting to the South
16. Quoted in Marc McCutcheon, *The Writer's Guide to Everyday Life in the 1800s*. Cincinnati: Writer's Digest Books, 1993, p. 71.
17. Quoted in McCutcheon, *The Writer's Guide to Everyday Life in the 1800s*, p. 86.
18. Olmsted, *The Cotton Kingdom*, p. 214.
19. Quoted in Jones, *The Plantation South*, p. 346.
20. Quoted in Jones, *The Plantation South*, p. 45.
21. Quoted in McCutcheon, *The Writer's Guide to Everyday Life in the 1800s*, p. 53.

Chapter 4: Visiting Plantations
22. Quoted in Robert Wernick, "Fanny Kemble Wins the Civil War: After Four Months on St. Simons Island,"

Glynn County, Georgia, Web site, www.glynncounty.com/History_and_Lore/Fanny_Kemble.

23. Quoted in Jones, *The Plantation South*, p. 382.
24. Quoted in Jones, *The Plantation South*, p. 370.
25. Olmsted, *The Cotton Kingdom*, p. 12.
26. Olmsted, *The Cotton Kingdom*, p. 250.
27. Quoted in Jones, *The Plantation South*, p. 61.
28. Quoted in Jones, *The Plantation South*, p. 126.
29. Quoted in John Shelton Reed and Dale Volberg Reed, *1001 Things Everyone Should Know About the South*. New York: Doubleday, 1996, p. 197.
30. Quoted in Stephen Currie, *Life of a Slave on a Southern Plantation*. San Diego: Lucent, 2000, p. 34.
31. Quoted in Jones, *The Plantation South*, p. 327.

Chapter 5: Exploring Rural Southern Culture
32. Olmsted, *The Cotton Kingdom*, p. 67.
33. Quoted in Jones, *The Plantation South*, p. 315.
34. Quoted in Jones, *The Plantation South*, p. 107.
35. Quoted in Simpkins, *A History of the South*, p. 137.
36. Quoted in McCutcheon, *The Writer's Guide to Everyday Life in the 1800s*, p. 13.
37. Quoted in McCutcheon, *The Writer's Guide to Everyday Life in the 1800s*, p. 24.
38. Quoted in Jones, *The Plantation South*, p. 44.
39. Quoted in Jones, *The Plantation South*, p. 304.
40. Quoted in McCutcheon, *The Writer's Guide to Everyday Life in the 1800s*, p. 180.
41. Olmsted, *The Cotton Kingdom*, p. 287.
42. Quoted in Jones, *The Plantation South*, p. 322.

Chapter 6: Exploring the South's Major Cities
43. Quoted in Reed and Reed, *1001 Things Everyone Should Know About the South*, p. 263.
44. Quoted in Reed and Reed, *1001 Things Everyone Should Know About the South*, p. 212.
45. Walter J. Fraser Jr., *Charleston! Charleston! The History of a Southern City*. Columbia: University of South Carolina Press, 1989, p. 229.
46. Olmsted, *The Cotton Kingdom*, p 37.
47. Quoted in McCutcheon, *The Writer's Guide to Everyday Life in the 1800s*, p. 180.
48. Olmsted, *The Cotton Kingdom*, p. 33.
49. Olmsted, *The Cotton Kingdom*, p. 213.

For Further Reading

Books

Stephen Currie, *Life of a Slave on a Southern Plantation*. San Diego: Lucent, 2000. The slave experience is related through words and pictures in this book for young adult readers.

Paul Erickson, *Daily Life on a Southern Plantation*. New York: Lodestar, 1998. With many illustrations and photographs of plantation-era artifacts, this beautiful picture book tells a detailed story of a day in the life of the Waverly Plantation in Louisiana.

James P. Reger, *Life in the South During the Civil War*. San Diego: Lucent, 1997. This book for young adults provides a detailed and accurate view of the sweeping changes that occurred in Southern society when the Civil War ended the antebellum period.

Harriet Beecher Stowe, *Uncle Tom's Cabin*. Pleasantville, NY: Reader's Digest Association, 1991. Originally published in 1852. This novel from fierce Northern abolitionist Stowe was perhaps the strongest antislavery tract ever published. Creating a huge stir in America of the 1850s, it was the most widely discussed book of its day among travelers and Southerners.

Web Sites

Monticello, the Home of Thomas Jefferson (www.monticello.org). This is a Web site devoted to information and events at Jefferson's Virginia estate.

Plank Roads (www.nchalloffame.com/plankroads.htm). From the North Carolina Hall of Fame's Web site, this North Carolina historical Web site has a great deal of information about the early years of the Tar Heel State.

Shirley Plantation (www.shirleyplantation.com). This Web site provides information, directions, and tour information for the oldest plantation in the nation.

Works Consulted

Books

John W. Blassingame, *The Slave Community: Plantation Life in the AnteBellum South.* New York: Oxford University Press, 1972. Constructed from verbal histories of former slaves, this book is an in-depth study of slave life.

Walter J. Fraser Jr., *Charleston! Charleston! The History of a Southern City.* Columbia: University of South Carolina Press, 1989. This is a very detailed and well-researched history of Charleston's early years, with information culled from rare early documents.

Katharine M. Jones, *The Plantation South.* Indianapolis: The Bobbs-Merrill Company, 1957. This delightful collection of letters from people who lived and traveled in the antebellum South brings the era to life through personal observances and descriptions of Southern lives and lifestyles.

Isabella G. Leland, *Charleston, Crossroads of History.* Woodland Hills, CA: Windsor, 1980. This is a scholarly study of Charleston history.

Marc McCutcheon, *The Writer's Guide to Everyday Life in the 1800s.* Cincinnati: Writer's Digest, 1993. This is a fine reference book with hundreds of entries that provide specific period detail of nineteenth-century America.

William S. McFeely, *Frederick Douglass.* New York: W.W. Norton, 1991. This is a thoughtful and eloquent biography of the great orator who escaped slavery and became one of the first and most passionate advocates of African American rights.

Frederick Law Olmsted, *The Cotton Kingdom: A Traveller's Observations on Cotton and Slavery.* New York: Alfred A. Knopf, 1953. This book is a fascinating and indispensable account of the author's journeys through the South in the 1850s. Olmsted is better known for his pioneering work as a landscape architect, including the design for New York City's Central Park.

John Shelton Reed and Dale Volberg Reed, *1001 Things Everyone Should Know About the South*. New York: Doubleday, 1996. The authors provide lively, fun guide to Southern life, a must-read for anyone interested in today's South.

Henry Savage Jr., *Discovering America 1700–1875*. New York: Harper & Row, 1979. This scholarly study of pioneering diaries and journeys focuses on the discovery of America's natural history, with accounts not only of southern explorations but also the westward journeys of Lewis and Clark and other pioneers.

Francis Butler Simkins, *A History of the South*. New York: Alfred A. Knopf, 1963. This is an excellent, well-documented history of the South from before European contact to post–Civil War reconstruction.

Jeffrey C. Stewart, *1001 Things Everyone Should Know About African American History*. New York: Doubleday, 1996. This interesting look at African American history in a digest form includes lots of biographical information about prominent blacks throughout history.

Henry Wiencek, *Plantations of the Old South*. Birmingham, AL: Oxmoor House, 1988. This handsome picture book conveys the beauty and charm of the South's surviving plantation homes.

Periodicals and Internet Sources

George Howe Colt, "Ghosts of the Mississippi," *Travel + Leisure*, March 2004.

Ashton Jung, "Creole in Black and White," Loyola University New Orleans, 1999. www.loyno.edu/~tlkinnon/Creoles.htm.

Robert Wernick, "Fanny Kemble Wins the Civil War: After Four Months on St. Simons Island," Glynn County, Georgia, Web site. www.glynncounty.com/History_and_Lore/Fanny_Kemble.

Index

Picture Credits

Cover photo: Charles Giroux, American, 1850s–1880s; Cotton Plantation, 1850s; Oil on canvas; Museum of Fine Arts, Boston; Gift of Maxim Karolik for the M. and M. Karolik Collection of American Paintings, 1815–1865; © 2005 Museum of Fine Arts, Boston. All rights reserved.

Art Explosion/Nova Development Corporation, 9, 10, 12, 13, 20, 22, 25, 30, 32, 34, 38, 43, 57, 62, 72, 74, 78, 90, 93

Art Resource, NY, 24

© Bettmann/CORBIS, 14, 16, 36, 42, 46, 68, 70, 71, 89

© Brooklyn Museum of Art, New York, USA/www.bridgeman.co.uk, 31

Brown Brothers, 7

© CORBIS, 52, 80, 88

Culver Pictures, 77

Getty Images, 41

Marie Hansen/Time Life Pictures/Getty Images, 96

Hulton Archive/Getty Images, 59, 85, 92

Illustrations of World-Famous Places, Dover Publications, 51

Library of Congress, 18, 23, 73

© Francis G. Mayer/CORBIS, 48

© Museum of Fine Arts, Boston, Massachusetts, USA/bridgeman.co.uk, 29

© Museum of the City of New York/CORBIS, 39

© New-York Historical Society, New York, USA/www.bridgeman.co.uk, 8

The New York Public Library/Art Resource, NY, 44

North Wind Picture Archives, 11, 17, 33, 64, 66, 75, 84, 94, 97

© Owaki - Kulla/CORBIS, 56

Réunion des Musées Nationaux/Art Resource, NY, 21, 54

Silhouettes, Dover Publications, 49, 65 (both), 87

© G.E. Kidder Smith/CORBIS, 55

Snark, Art Resource, NY, 61

Transportation, Dover Publications 44

Weapons and Armor, Dover Publications, 45

Steve Zmina, 58

About the Author

Jim Gullo is a writer who lives on an island in the Pacific Northwest. He enjoys travel, golf, scuba diving, and jumping on a trampoline with his two sons, Michael and Joe. He has written hundreds of articles for magazines about travel throughout the world, and his book credits for young-adult and adult readers include *The Importance of Hillary Rodham Clinton, Just Let Me Play: The Story of Charlie Sifford*, and *Seattle & the Olympic Peninsula for Dummies*.